Secret Society

The Illuminati

Separating

Fact from Fiction

Conrad Bauer

Copyrights

Disclaimer and Terms of Use

ISBN: 978-1534751095

Printed in the United States

MAPLEWOOD
— PUBLISHING —

Contents

Introduction

The Illuminati dominate any discussion of secret societies. Search the web, spark up a conversation, or search through a library shelf and soon enough you will encounter their name. They have become an ancient order and a modern sensation at the same time. They are at once a ubiquitous herald of the new world order and the people who market pop albums, and trying to discern the truth about the organization can get lost amid the hail of noise that inevitably follows any mention of their name. In this book, we hope to do something different. Here we will try to separate fact from fiction and confront the truth about the Illuminati.

In order to achieve this, we have uncovered fifteen of the most frequently asked questions, queries, and accusations that people have relating to the Illuminati. By taking a discerning, informed look at each of these ideas in detail, we will be able to reach the truth that so many people seek but which can be so hard to find. If you have ever wanted a handy guide to cutting through the mess of information that you find online, then this guide will be perfect for you.

Throughout the course of this book, we will look into the origins of the Illuminati, their involvement with the Freemasons, accusations of Satanism thrown at them, the idea that the caused the French Revolution, their involvement with ancient and celebrity cultures, and their appearance on the dollar bill of the United States of America. If you have ever wanted to know the truth about the Illuminati in a simple, easy-to-understand guide, this book is exactly what you need.

The Illuminati and Their Origins

It makes sense to start at the beginning. Even when discussing the early origins of the Illuminati, a cursory glance at the range of sources out there will provide the reader with a hundred different answers. Some say that the society started life in Ancient Egypt, others say that they did not become a real force until the establishment of the United States of America. In this guide, however, we want to discover the provable truth. In this regard, it should be stated for the record that – in spite of the protestations of some people – there is a degree of truth to the Illuminati story. They began life as a legitimate secret society, one with big plans and a restricted membership. So before we go on to look at a few of the more disputed stories surrounding the society, we should take the time to outline exactly what we know and exactly what we can prove. To do this, we will need to travel to Bavaria, Germany, in the 18th Century.

Though the name might have taken on new meaning in the modern age (a point which we shall return to later), the original Illuminati were not only a very real and very secret society, but they really existed, and we can legitimately verify it. In fact, their history has been passed down to us over the course of several centuries. Rather than providing insight into a domineering global conspiracy, the history of the Bavarian group can demonstrate to us how the politics and beliefs of the European Enlightenment were put into practice. Rather than being built on the occult, the strange, and the mysterious, the Illuminati of the 18th Century were formed with very scholarly principles in mind. The story of how they came into being, however, means taking a tour of the halls of German academia of the time.

One of the most important names in this story is Adam Weishaupt, who was working at the time as a professor as the University of Ingolstadt. His specialties were Practical Philosophy and Common Law, giving us something of an indication that he was something of a down-to-earth man. He was not, however, surrounded by likeminded individuals. The University of Ingolstadt was known to be a predominantly Jesuit institution. The Jesuits – particularly devout and scholarly Catholics – occupied almost every position, to the point where Weishaupt was the only professor who did not count himself among their number. Though ostensibly dissolved in 1773, the Jesuit order continued to endure against the shifting praxis of the Catholic Church. The University was one of their most important institutions and – even if their name was not officially still above the door – they very much controlled the finances for the school.

Figure 1 - Adam Weishaupt

The Jesuits were defined by their devotion to the Christian cause. Unfortunately for them, this was a post reformation world. The efforts of Martin Luther and his fellow reformists had been particularly fruitful in Germany, leading the Catholics – and, in particular, the Jesuits – into difficult times. Fighting to retain control of one of the last bastions of their power, there was a marked effort within the University to discredit and ostracize any member of staff who was not a member of the Order. Weishaupt was clearly one such person, and his future at the University was seemingly doomed. Anything that was deemed to be in any way liberal or even Protestant was deeply abhorred by the Jesuits, and it is perhaps because of this that Weishaupt found himself pushing back against the institution's ideals with such vigor. He became a consummate preacher of the ideals of the Enlightenment, promoting reason, liberty, progress, and constitutional government as the future. It was a worldview that left little room for the Catholic Church and their teachings. It was inevitable that Weishaupt would find himself in trouble.

However, he was a clever man. Knowing that there was little to be done through soapbox style preaching, Weishaupt decided that he would conduct his affairs in a far more secretive manner. As the idea of forming a secret society grew more and more appealing with each passing day, the professor began to consider potential members for his new group, searching for compatible people who were already in and around the University of Ingolstadt.

One of his first considerations was turning to the Freemasons. We will cover the links between the Freemasons and the Illuminati in greater depth in coming chapters, but their organization structure and secretive approach seemed to be directly in line with the kind of group Weishaupt was hoping to form. There was, however, a major issue. Membership of the Freemasons was a costly endeavor. It would require a fortune to operate such a group under their banner. Weishaupt also felt that there might be ideological opposition from the already entrenched Freemasons. He had his own ideas about the world, his own philosophies, and some of these might clash directly with the way in which Freemasonry operated. Instead, Weishaupt quickly realized that he had little choice but to start his own organization, one which would be imbued with his Enlightenment ideals right from the very start.

That is not to say that Weishaupt could not draw influence from other people and other societies. In particular, he noted the way in which Freemasonry was organized along a grade system, with members increasing their knowledge and their involvement the closer they moved towards the higher echelons of the order. This seemed, to Weishaupt, to be an adept way of organizing those around him, and it would be perfect for the establishment of a clandestine group within the walls of the University. In order to remain hidden from the Jesuits and the rest of society, borrowing the structure of the Freemasons would allow him to conduct the group's business with a relative confidence in their hidden nature.

The first name Weishaupt considered was the Covenant of Perfectibility (Bund der Perfektibilisten, in the original German). It was under this name that Weishaupt and four carefully selected students from the University first met in 1776 on the 1st of May. Not only did they meet under the name of the Covenant of Perfectibility, but they collectively decided that they would employ the owl of Minerva as their sign. Being a secret society, they soon realized that aliases would be a useful addition to their group, settling on alternative names for all involved. Weishaupt himself became known as Spartacus, while others took names such as Ajax, Tiberius, Agathon, and Erasmus Roterodamus (who were otherwise known as Massenhausen, Merz, Bauhof, and Sutor, respectively). The latter member, Erasmus Roterodamus, would later be expelled from the group, with Weishaupt citing "indolence" as the reason. All of the students studied law and so were in close contact with and already known to Weishaupt. He could trust them, he believed, and he knew them to have similarly inclined political views.

So the Covenant of Perfectibility continued to meet for almost two years, until it was realized that the name was not ideal. It was quickly found that the title was too vague and too strange to function as the name for a potentially world-changing group. Weishaupt's next decision would have ramifications throughout the next few centuries, passing down to us a name that has become famous not only for its association with Weishaupt and his battle against the Jesuits, but one that has also become a hallmark of popular culture. One of the names briefly considered was "the Bee Order," though this was soon rejected. It needed to be not only grandiose and intimidating but also reflective of the group's learned status. And so, in 1778, in the month of April, the group officially retitled itself as the Order of Illuminati (Illuminatenorden in German).

And, just like that, the Illuminati were born. As we will see later in this book, it was not simple sailing from there on out. Weishaupt's efforts to popularize and expand his society would prove to be difficult, with arguments, encounters, and rival groups emerging alongside the Illuminati. However, we can depend on these facts for the very essence of our study into the history of the Illuminati. There are papers and accounts of the group's meeting that are extant to this day, providing documented proof that the Order of Illuminati not only existed, but that it also was established in an 18th Century German University. All of these factors will come to be important when we address questions that appear later in this book, though for now it is very useful in dispelling a number of key misinterpretations about the origin of the Illuminati.

First, the Order of the Illuminati is not referenced in documents, writings, recorded text, or any other kind of scripture before the events of 1778. As such, it is quite easy to counteract against claims that the Illuminati are an ancient secret society that only rose to the surface in the 18th Century. That the group formed by Weishaupt was, at one point, operating under a different name, demonstrates that the title of Illuminati was not an elder group, risen up from the depths of history. It was a creation of the German law professor, but it would prove to be a significant one. As we will see in later chapters, there have been efforts to attribute the Illuminate's existence to a number of iconographical signifiers found through ancient, medieval, and Renaissance art, though these are typically without any foundation. That we have such well-organized and collected accounts of the formation of the Order of Illuminati allows anyone with an evidence-based, empirical, value system to point at a specific juncture in German history as the birth point of the Illuminati.

The second point to counter is the suggestion, less common, that the Illuminati are an American invention. As we have already seen, the year of 1776 was important in the founding of the Illuminati. The group shares this in common with the United States of America, whose history hails July the 4th, 1776 as being the day the country became officially independent from Great Britain. Many have pointed to this slight parallel as being justification enough to suggest collusion between Weishaupt and the American forefathers. However, this is rampant speculation. There exists no evidence of any communication between any of the American leaders at the time and Weishaupt. Furthermore, the name Illuminati was not actually created until two years later. During the formative years of Weishaupt's organization, it is safe to say that men such as George Washington and Thomas Jefferson had more important concerns that a small, unheralded, secret society hidden within the walls of a Jesuit university.

That is not to say that they might not have been interested, however. It has been a long-documented fact that the founding fathers of the United States were heavily interested in the principles of the European Enlightenment. The influence can be read in the Declaration of Independence and the Constitution. Many of the ideals that the founding fathers were attempting to imbue in their nascent country were shared by Weishaupt, the kind of principles he wished to spread through the Jesuit-dominated University. Had the two groups (the founding fathers and the Order of Illuminati) sat down around a dinner table, it would not likely have been long before they discovered common ideological ground. While it is an entirely unsupported and almost impossible possibility that the men who helped founded the United States also formed the Illuminati, we can at least concede that there do exist parallels between the two groups. The key difference, however, lies in the fact that Weishaupt's society chose to operate in the shadows, while George Washington et al were very vocal in their defiance.

Thanks to the evidence that we have gathered together, we can place an almost exact starting point on the history of the Illuminati. But as we will see in the next chapter, this history can quickly become complicated.

The Illuminati Are a Secret Sect of Freemasons

It is impossible to understand the history of the Illuminati without mentioning the Freemasons. As one of the most successful secret societies ever conceived, the Freemasons have entered into the popular public consciousness in a way few other organizations have managed. They have outposts all over the world, with these so-called Lodges being found in North America, Europe, the Middle East, and many other places. Often associated with wealth and strange rituals, their organization is said to be built on the accruing of ancient knowledge, ideas that are then used to increase influence and power throughout the world. Many secret societies, whether real or mythical, have been linked with the Freemasons at one point or another. Likewise, many conspiracy theories posit that the Freemasons are the power behind the curtain, influencing events around the world. The Illuminati are no different. But are the Illuminati actually a secret sect of the Freemasons?

The answer is not straightforward, though there are indications that the two organizations have become very intertwined at various points in their histories. More than most, the Illuminati have taken ideas, members, and attention away from the Freemasons, an exchange that has also occurred in the opposite direction. While the answer to many of these questions of fact and fiction regarding the Illuminati can be difficult to answer, there is little doubt that there is a tangible bond between the Freemasons and the Illuminati as they existed in the 18th Century. In order to discover exactly what this bond entailed, we will need to delve once again into the history of the Bavarian order.

After founding the Order of Illuminati, Weishaupt and his fellow members faced one major problem: how to bring more people into the fold. As the University of Ingolstadt was a Jesuit institution, recruiting from the student body was tough and recruiting from the faculty even harder. So it fell on one of the students to handle the bulk of the recruiting work. Massenhausen (Ajax, as he was known) was the most active, especially as he left Ingolstadt a short time after the group was founded. He went to study in Munich, which proved a rich pool of resources. One of the most significant Illuminati recruits was a man named Xavier von Zwack, who had studied under Weishaupt previously. Von Zwack was embarking on a career in administration, so he would provide the group with an insight into government in the region, especially into the Bavarian National Lottery, where the new recruit was now plying his trade.

Despite the success Massenhausen found in recruiting new Illuminati members, this success quickly soured. Weishaupt began to view the swelling ranks of the Order as a threat, with the student seemingly selecting candidates that were later deemed to be unsuitable. This would later be compounded by a somewhat erratic approach to romantic relationships, an issue that meant Weishaupt could rely little on Massenhausen. In order to remedy the situation, Weishaupt decided that the Munich outpost of the Illuminati should come under new leadership. He trusted Von Zwack to head up what was quickly becoming an important branch of the Order. The civil servant agreed, but soon discovered that Massenhausen's unreliability had been far worse than previously thought. The man had been misappropriating the subscription funds paid by members and had even been reading the private communications between Weishaupt and his former pupil. Accordingly, Massenhausen left the Order of the Illuminati in 1778. Having graduated from Ingolstadt, he took a position in a different region of Germany and resigned himself to having nothing to do with the group. As there were only twelve members by this point, he likely considered himself to be missing out on very little.

Following this period, Von Zwack took on the mantle of chief recruiter. His actions proved more successful, especially as he attempted to bring in a number of more influential and mature people. Of these, Weishaupt was pleased to see a man named Hertel come into the organization. Hertel had been a childhood friend and was now a canon of the government body, the Munich Frauenkirche. By 1778, as the group changed its name to the Order of Illuminati, membership numbers were up to around twenty-seven. They could be found in a number of different German cities, such as Ingolstadt, Munich, Ravensberg, Freysingen, and Eichstaedt. All of them were given codenames, taken from the cities of Ancient Greece.

But how does this relate to the Freemasons? As the ranks of the Order swelled, Weishaupt decided that he would organize the membership along Masonic lines. For example, there were three grades of involvement. These were Novice, Minerval, and the Illuminated Minerval. These were roughly equivalent to the way in which Freemason lodges organized involvement, in which they assigned (and still assign) members to categories of Apprentice, Journeyman, and Master

Mason. Just as in the Freemasons, moving up through the ranks would bring greater insight into the knowledge possessed by the group. In addition, each movement up a rank would be accompanied by something akin to social advancement. When reaching the stage of Illuminated Minerval, the member would finally be shown the technical secrets of the organization, including the secret handshakes, signs, and passwords that provided entry into the innermost circles. This was a structure borrowed almost wholesale from Freemasonry.

Freemasonry is an often misunderstood phenomenon. The origins of the group can be traced back as far the 14th Century, with the Freemasons themselves presenting (and often mythologized) version of their history in their own Old Charges, a collection of historical documents. The Freemasons have for their symbol a compass and square, a logo that can be seen adorning buildings around the world. Walk through any capital country (especially in Europe or the United States) and you will eventually come across the symbol, often carved into stone above a doorway. With members including everyone from local architects to American presidents, the Freemasons are usually well represented at the highest levels. The stories one hears about the Masons can often be deceiving. As with the Illuminati, they find themselves at the center of many mistruths and false attributions (though that is the subject for another book.) Just as with the Illuminati, there is the suggestions of a secret order quietly pulling the strings from the shadows. But the truth of the matter is that – whatever the Freemasons once were – they rarely amount to little more than a social club in today's world. Often joined by businessmen, the influential, and the upwardly mobile, the Masons and their Lodges function as a meeting place for likeminded people. The organizations are networking clubs, akin to social media for the pre-internet age. Introductions are made, relationships struck up. On a local level, the Lodges serve as a means of putting compatible people in touch for a mutual benefit.

However, the Freemasons are an organization with a great deal of history, and this history can imbue the modern iterations with a seemingly archaic quality. Similarly, at the time when the Illuminati were first discovering how best to organize themselves, the 18th Century Freemasons provided them with a social template. As the Freemasons were a very old society, they had a number of pre-Enlightenment rituals and ceremonies that had been passed down over the years. Many of these rituals are still held today, especially when a member passing from one rank into the next. In the course of moving up through the ranks, a Mason might first swear to fulfil a number of obligations to his Lodge. From there onwards, he might swear to keep the secrets of the Freemasons from both outsiders and those of a lower rank. He will be provided with literature and an opportunity to look into a number of private historical objects that the Masons have preserved. But strangest of all is the fact that some of the Freemasons often include more occult and outlandish rituals. As well as the compass and square, other objects such as the trowel, the level, and the plumb rule are also incorporated into the ceremonies, as well as a so-called moral lesson. These rituals and ceremonies are ostensibly secret, though a number have been revealed and even filmed. To the outsider, not aware of the actions' allegorical meanings, they can appear strange and almost occult. But the truth is that they are often harmless and – at least in the modern age – something akin to theatre. By the time Weishaupt and his followers began to take note of the Masons and their rituals, the ancient wisdom that these rituals were said to represent had long since been forgotten. Instead, their actions mirrored the Freemasons in other ways.

Just as with the Freemasons, the Illuminati began to limit their recruitment strategies to people who fit within a select few demographics. All men were expected to be Christian (as was essentially standard at the time), and people such as Pagans or Jews were expressly prohibited. Alongside these religious requirements, the Illuminati also forbade membership to monks, women, and those who were involved with any other secret society. Ideally, every single recruit would fit into the same description. That is, they would be between the ages of 18 and 30, financially well-off, docile, and willing to expand their knowledge. With the majority of the recruits coming from current and former university students, membership of the Illuminati was quickly drawn along very set and somewhat privileged lines.

However, as the Illuminati expanded, Weishaupt found that he needed to keep tabs on his growing ranks. This was achieved by a system of counter-espionage, in which certain members spied on other members. Weishaupt was at the center, with many different people feeding him information, often without realizing that they themselves were being recorded. Those who were the most trusted were welcomed into the inner circle, a ruling council that was also known as Areopagus. When selected novices were given permission to go out and recruit, they were given the title of Insinuants.

But recruiting became difficult. The Order's rule requiring members not be involved in other secret societies, in particular, proved to be tough. On several occasions, Weishaupt had to step in to convince his recruits not to join the far larger and more influential Freemasons. This became such an issue that Weishaupt decided that he would join the Freemasons himself in order to gather information for the betterment of the Illuminati. So, rather than the Illuminati emerging from a sect of the Freemasons, the early history of Weishaupt's Order was marked by the difficulty that the Freemasons caused.

Weishaupt moved through the Freemasons' earliest ranks quickly. The Blue Lodge's three degrees (early steps along the path of Freemasonry) passed by with very little noteworthy information. By 1778, Von Zwack was also beginning to conduct research into the secrets of the Freemasons in the hope of benefitting the Illuminati. He came into contact with a man named Abbé Marotti, who claimed to be a priest with a good knowledge of the higher echelons of Masonry. According to Marotti, the secret knowledge of the Freemasons was related to ancient religions and the very earliest years of the church. It was enough to convince Von Zwack that there was more to the Freemasons than a simple structural quality that could be gained. He reached out to Weishaupt and advised that the two secret societies should join their forces or at least enjoy a friendly relationship. By the end of 1778, Weishaupt's lack of success in moving up through the ranks, as well as the information from the priest, led to a changed attitude within the Illuminati. They decided to establish a Lodge of their own.

Such was the organizational structure of the Freemasons that setting up a Lodge was almost like setting up a franchise. Weishaupt and his fellow Illuminati sent a warrant to the Grand Lodge located in Prussia – the regional headquarters, so to speak – and after a small array of difficulties, were eventually permitted to establish their own Masonic Lodge. They named it Theodore of the Good Council, a name chosen specifically to flatter and appeal to Charles Theodore, the Elector of Bavaria. The Lodge was founded in 1779, and in no time, the members were almost entirely Illuminati.

Within a few months, the Illuminati had total control of the Masonic outpost. Their next goal was to ensure that they would be able to operate independently, free from the instructions passed down by the Grand Lodge. To do this, Weishaupt and his fellow members put themselves in touch with other Lodges around Germany. In doing so, they built up relationships that eventually allowed them to operate outside of the influence of the Grand Lodge and to be recognized in their own right. They used clever internal politics and machinations to surgically remove themselves from the main Masonic host. Once it had been declared independent – and this independence recognized by other Lodges –the Theodore of the Good Council (which was, by now, just another name for the Illuminati) was permitted to create and run smaller Lodges whenever they pleased. The franchise was now allowed to create new franchises in their own self-image.

So why is this important, and how does it tie the Illuminati to the Freemasons? It should be stated at this stage that the Freemasons were a far larger, continent-wide concern. What was happening in some remote region of Germany was likely of little interest to the men running the Freemasons. But what the Masons did have was a structure and an operating organizational body. This allowed them to recruit and provided them with some form of acceptable existence. Though many countries had outlawed secret societies, the Freemasons had enough history that most people – at least, those who might be recruited – were at least aware of their existence. This kind of authenticity was something Weishaupt and his Illuminati lacked. Having seen the Freemasons operate in such a way, the Illuminati coveted the rival organization. Weishaupt's plan was essentially parasitic. Moving in under the guise of joining the club, the Illuminati adjoined themselves to the host body, fed off the structural and recruiting benefits of the organization, and used the Freemasons to make themselves stronger. Once they felt suitably empowered, the Illuminati began to break away and grow increasingly independent. While there might have been esoteric designs on ancient knowledge held within the Masonic walls, it was the functionality, the resources, and the reputation that the Illuminati truly lacked. Weishaupt's group already had an ideology and an ethos. What they lacked was the ability to put these ideas into practice. By siphoning away their needs from the Freemasons, the Illuminati were able to maneuver their own society into a greater, more powerful position.

As such, there might be some truth to the idea that the Illuminati are a secret sect of the Freemasons. Certainly, at a pivotal moment in the history of Weishaupt's Order, the Illuminati were very much tied to their own Masonic Lodge. They existed and operated within the Freemasons, using the platform for their own benefit. But while this is true, it is important to note that the

Freemasons were often little aware of what was happening. To tie the two groups together would be dishonest. At the time, the Illuminati were like the mosquito sitting on the neck of the sleeping man. The man might notice, wave his hand in the direction of some minor irritation, and then roll over and fall back asleep. Once the mosquito has taken its fill, it would simply fly away. At the time, the Illuminati were incomparable to the Freemasons. But at the time, all they needed was a small boost in order to raise their profile and recruit men like Adolph Knigge. As we will see in later chapters, Masonic recruits such as Knigge would help determine the course of the Illuminati in the coming years. This sharing of recruits and structural organizations would be the biggest gift imparted to the Illuminati from the Freemasons and would be their biggest point of comparison. It would not be, however, a long term relationship.

The Illuminati Guard an Ancient Secret

As with the majority of conspiracy theories, many of the stories told about the Illuminati depend on secrets. If the old adage is true, then knowledge is power. Some people take this further, suggesting that the most powerful secret societies in the history of the world have held on to some great hidden truth that grants them exceptional influence. It is said of the Knights Templar, who supposedly excavated a buried treasure on Jerusalem's Temple Mount during the Crusades. It has been said of the Priory of Sion, who supposedly guarded the secret of the extant descendants of Jesus Christ, before they were proven to be a small-time hoax blown out of proportion. And it had been said many times about the Freemasons, who supposedly guarded great secrets that were made known to only the highest ranking members of the organization.

In the case of the Freemasons, this is likely due to the way in which the society came into the world. One need only look at the name of the society itself to discover that "Masons" is not just a title. During the Medieval period, when the first rumblings of organization were gathering in European cities, masons were important people. Roughly equivalent to today's architects, they guarded the knowledge required to build the most impressive of buildings. These mathematical doctrines told members how to cut stone properly and how to construct a load-bearing wall. In a time when society was largely illiterate, these ideas were almost magic in their execution. And because they were trade secrets, they were not just passed along to anyone. Almost like a modern union, the

Masons gathered together and shared the techniques of their craft. To learn them, one would first need to be an apprentice, a journeyman, and then a master. As time went on and more and more people were admitted to the ranks, these traditional secrets took on a more allegorical quality. The compass and square that are still the logo of the Freemasons are no longer just tools of the trade, but rather represent the ideals of knowledge and logic that the Masons hold dear. While they might have once been a closely guarded secret, they served to form the basis of the Order before taking on a more mystical meaning in later life.

So how does this affect the Illuminati? At the time we left them, they were beginning to infiltrate the ranks of Freemasonry. Having established their own independent Lodge, they were closer than ever to the central knowledge possessed by the Freemasons. But still Weishaupt was not satisfied. Having joined the Freemasons and found nothing mystical that would help his own secret society, he began to turn the majority of his attention back towards the Illuminati. Besides, the Illuminati had their own ideals to guard. They were founded on their own traditions and ideologies. Formed on the principles of the Age of Enlightenment, the Freemasons' ancient proclivity for architecture might have seemed altogether more practical for a professor of Civic Law and philosophy.

This is where Adolph Knigge comes into the story. Having been one of the recruits who came into the Illuminati in 1780, he had been a Freemason with big ideas. Having joined the older society and sped through the ranks, he had been filled with dramatic ideas and innovations that he thought could be implemented.

When he reached the higher ranks of Freemasonry, his disappointment was palpable. Any plans that he suggested for reform and modernization were quickly rejected. This is when he met Costanzo Marchese di Costanzo, already a member of the Illuminati and one of the order's best recruiters. He noticed Adolph Knigge's disappointment in the Freemasons and let him in on a secret: the kind of plans Knigge possessed were already being put into motion in certain secret circles. A short time later, Knigge had been recruited into the Illuminati.

Figure 2 - Adolph Freiherr Knigge

Rather than the Freemasons initiations, which typically hinted towards their technical past, the entrance materials for the Illuminati were decidedly more intellectual. At the time, the very idea of liberal literature was outlawed in Bavaria (and indeed, many other regions of Europe). Some of the most progressive ideas that were born out of the Enlightenment were illegal. In certain Protestant countries, these materials were widely circulated. They offered criticism of the Catholic Church, as well as other Enlightenment writings on matters such as liberty and an opposition to absolute monarchy. They promoted science, empiricism, and a questioning of the surrounding world. It is easy to see why such materials might be deemed detrimental to the Bavarian state. But for anyone interested in joining the Illuminati, for those men who had demonstrated themselves as being open to such ideas, these were the mystical ideas that lay at the center of the Illuminati and marked them out as being a dangerous and almost revolutionary group. Knigge, along with a number of his close friends, seemed to be open to such ideas.

One of the best recruiting grounds for the early Illuminati members was the young, disillusioned men who found society too traditional and unwilling to change. Secret societies offered them the potential means by which they could meet and discuss such reforms. Before the internet age or the rise of the mass media, such meetings were incredibly valuable. To the state, they were incredibly dangerous. For most people, the Freemasons were the most obvious choice of secret society, almost the ubiquitous name that was commonly associated with the very idea of a secret society. But as we have seen with Knigge, the size of the organization was often its undoing. As there were so many Freemasons, it was harder to chart a course into more revolutionary waters. In order to accomplish that, one would have to join a society that was founded on the very principles that Knigge and similarly minded men were hoping to promote. They would need to join the Illuminati.

As such, the literature which Costanzo provided was the Illuminati's material for passing into the Minerval grade. Though the materials proved distasteful to Knigge's three companions, Knigge himself discovered exactly what he was looking for. Rather than an ancient secret or traditional mysticism that many people associate with the Illuminati in the modern age, the group was instead founded on progressive and somewhat radical ideas. These were illegal ideas, dangerous philosophies, but to a man like Knigge, they seemed to be the future. There is a truth to the idea that the Illuminati were built on a secret, but it is false to describe that secret as ancient. Instead, the Enlightenment principles discussed within the clandestine walls of the Illuminati were on the cutting edge of contemporary philosophy.

Knigge's recruitment was important for a number of reasons. While we might not know the exact materials he read (only their nature), it demonstrates the kind of person to whom the Illuminati seemed appealing. In many respects, he was the quintessential recruit for Weishaupt's order. Young, scholarly, rich, and with a desire to discuss very important ideas, Knigge would almost become the poster boy for Illuminati membership. As well as this, however, it was important for the effect that Knigge would have upon the Order in the coming years. Knigge himself was somewhat flattered by being welcomed into the Illuminati. The society's attentions were something of a compliment and a confirmation of the ideas he had developed privately. He appreciated the principles on which the Illuminati were built, namely a quest to educate the people of the world and protect them from the despotism of monarchy.

However, in addition to these founding ideals, Weishaupt met with Knigge and the two discussed other subjects. While Knigge talked about plans for reforming groups such as the Freemasons, he also convinced Weishaupt of the benefits of the so-called "higher sciences," such as alchemy. By the end of their discussions, Weishaupt threw his support behind Knigge, and quickly the new recruit found his position within the society rising exponentially. But in order to break into the highest ranks, Knigge would have to prove himself. Weishaupt set him the challenge of recruiting new members of exceptional quality. Knigge agreed, but only on the basis that he would be allowed to select where the recruits were taken from. When everything was agreed, Knigge returned, once again, to the Freemasons.

By now, it was clear that the Freemasons were a fertile source of recruits. While Freemasonry might have once possessed a secret cadre of knowledge, Knigge was able to recruit people to the Illuminati by revealing to them the most current and progressive materials around at the time. The Illuminati were the future, the coming order of things. At the time, however, there was a problem. In an effort to give the Illuminati some degree of credibility, Weishaupt had constructed an elaborate back story for the group. This information was said to be made available to the highest ranking members of the groups, though snippets were teased to potential new recruits. Weishaupt outlined this history to Knigge, telling him about the "Most Serene Superiors," a seemingly cosmic force whom the Illuminati served, along with a fictitious history of the Order that stretched back long before the real founding date. Knigge, though mostly successful in his recruitment, found the stories hard to remember. It was something of an embarrassment when the new poster boy for the Illuminati could not recall their supposed history.

Not deterred by Knigge's inability to impart the Illuminati's invented past, Weishaupt looked upon the recruitment he conducted as largely successful; so much so that he tasked Knigge with creating and executing one of the Order's first real actions: the distribution of a pamphlet that detailed the continued existence and practice of the Jesuits. The pamphlet showed the reader how the supposedly outlawed Jesuits were still in fact preaching and practicing in Bavaria. It was the first time that the Illuminati crossed over and made an impact on the world outside of their internal discussions. Knigge was satisfied with the work in distributing the pamphlet but wrote to Weishaupt in 1781 admitting to his own concern that he was unable to convincingly answer questions about the Illuminati's most mystical histories. As Weishaupt began to realize that he might lose Knigge and all the good work the man was doing, he admitted to having created the entire history. The "Most Serene Superiors" were an invention, the ancientness of the Illuminati was a construction, and many of the higher order of the society had not yet even been written.

This, more than anything else, can highlight the lack of an ancient secret that was being guarded by the Illuminati. There was certainly an awareness within the group that such inventions could prove to be useful, perhaps in a similar manner to the way in which the Freemasons used their history; an allegorical lesson. However, it did not sit well with the supposedly radical literature which the Illuminati themselves enjoyed. While it might have been expected that Knigge was shocked and appalled by such lies, he seemed to be quite the opposite. In fact, Weishaupt and Knigge discussed the matter calmly. Even with the revelation that he would not be learning some secret hidden truth belonging to the Masons or anything of the sort, Knigge was promised that he would be brought closer to the central power of the Illuminati. Alongside Weishaupt, he could read the original notes and help craft some of the ideas that would be passed down to those most trusted members. Knigge saw this as an opportunity to spread some of his own philosophies and ideas. As he claimed, these new ideas would make the Illuminati an even more attractive prospect for likeminded young Germans. As such, Knigge was given 50 florins by the Illuminati council (the Areopagus) and sent on what resembled a diplomatic mission.

By this point in the history of the Illuminati, it was clear to many people that there was no great secret hidden away in the coffers of the Illuminati. As we have traced their existence from its inception, we can be clear on such a matter. But for those who came late to the party – like Adolph Knigge – the matter was not so set in stone. With other organizations such as the Freemasons teasing potential recruits with the possibility that there might be some ancient occult secret that they will learn only when they reach the higher levels, the Illuminati seemed to be certain that they too should have this potential. But, as we have seen in the writing of Knigge, the entirety of the Illuminati history at this stage was a poorly built construction. It was one that Weishaupt or his Areopagus had not even bothered to finish. While there are suggestions in the modern age that the Illuminati were founded on some ancient principle, the truth is far more interesting. The order came into existence purely to propagate and further very new ideas. As we will see in coming chapters, such ideas would form the backbone of many of the accusations later levelled at the Illuminati. But in a much more immediate way, they would cause a great deal of internal strife. While there is no closely guarded historical secret behind the Illuminati, we will soon learn how they struggled to formulate their own future. Before one sets out to conquer the world, it helps to have one's affairs in order.

The Illuminati Control the World

Travelling as we are through the history of the Illuminati, it is time to confront one of the most enduring myths that circulates around the Order. While we have seen in previous chapters that some of the accusations levelled at the Illuminati do have merit and can at least be worth discussing, the idea that the Illuminati control the world is a very modern suggestion. As we will see in this chapter, they struggled at first to control their own members. Filled with internal conflicts, divisions in ideology, and disagreements over the future actions of the Order, it is important to see the Illuminati as a very human construct. Just like any other human construct, those within it are very prone to human failings. Rather than a single, driven entity that pulls the strings from the shadow, this chapter will reveal exactly how divided and difficult the members of the Illuminati found it to put their ideas into practice.

In 1780, just a few years after the original founding of the Illuminati, Weishaupt found himself in a difficult place. Though the order was still very much in its early stages, the membership numbers had grown well. For a secret society, they had managed to spread the word of their presence and were beginning to generate something of a reputation, at least in certain regions of Bavaria. However, there were divisions within the Illuminati. As the founder, Weishaupt might have expected total autonomy over the group. But the Areopagus did not agree. Those on the council seemed to find Weishaupt to be something of a dictator; his approach was inconsistent and marked by stubbornness. One of the only times he had offered to concede ground – when

Knigge looked like he might leave – proved to be the apparent solution. Knigge became something of a go-between and a peacemaker, talking to both the Areopagus and Weishaupt.

Knigge quickly realized that there were many problems within the Illuminati. If they were to advance as an organization, then Knigge would have to tackle such difficulties. The first of these lay in the recruitment policy. It should be quite obvious that the success of a secret society lives or dies on its recruitment tactics. Try to recruit too many people, and the authorities will quickly become aware. Try to recruit too few, and you run the risk of the group failing to grow. Recruit the wrong members, and you will find that the society is incapable of achieving its original goal. It becomes a difficult balancing act, which is why successful recruiters like Knigge were so appreciated, and unsuccessful recruiters like Massenhausen were quick to leave the order.

For his part, Welshaupt had placed an emphasis on recruiting university students. This is perhaps understandable for a professor in a Jesuit institution who saw his pupils as potential minds he could save on a regular basis. But the resulting effect of this strategy meant that many of the more senior positions within the Illuminati were quickly filled with bright, energetic, and enthusiastic young men who critically lacked any administrative experience. Instead of these younger recruits, the Areopagus felt that it would be better served by recruiting older, more experienced men, likely from the Freemasons. But therein lay a second problem. As Knigge saw it, those older and more experienced Freemasons would likely be perturbed by the Illuminati's anti-religious (specifically anti-Jesuit) stance. What had started as something of a distrust of the Jesuits had turned into a general anti-religious sentiment throughout many areas of the Illuminati.

Das

verbefferte Syftem

der

Illuminaten

mit allen

feinen Graden und Einrichtungen.

Herausgegeben von

Adam Weishaupt

Herzoglich Sachf. Goth. Hofrath.

Hic fitus eft Phaeton, currus auriga paterni:
Quem fi non tenuit; magnis tamen excidit aufis.
Ovid. Met. B. 2.

Neue und vermehrte Auflage.

Frankfurt und Leipzig,
in der Grattenauerifchen Buchhandlung. 1788.

Figure 3 - Illuminati pamphlet from 1788

It was a problem particular to Bavaria. In this part of Europe, the Catholics were still in control. Elsewhere, the Reformation had seen an upheaval in the way religion was practiced. While still technically Christian, the schism between Catholicism and Protestantism was huge. Many people died as a result of their beliefs. Wars were fought. To the anti-religious in the midst of Catholic-controlled Bavaria, such an opposition might seem justifiable, at least according to Knigge. But the people who the Areopagus hoped to recruit? The older, more influential men? They might be put off by such a stance. If the Illuminati hoped to spread beyond Bavaria, then this religious distaste would have to be tempered. Both Weishaupt and the Areopagus recognized the issues, but both found themselves with little solution other than to place their trust in Knigge to find a resolution. Thanks to the man's contacts, he could make inroads into Freemason recruitment, untainted by any obvious association with anti-religious views. He also possessed the ritualistic skill that was required in order to refine the grade structure of the Illuminati. They were still keen to make use of the Freemason's approach, but their efforts to write and build a progressive system of advancement within the order (including rituals for passing up a grade and so on) had ground to a halt. Knigge was given the task of writing and implementing these rituals, as well as going out into the wider world to head up the recruitment. There were a couple of conditions, in that he must submit his ritual ideas for approval and would need to discuss many of his choices before implementing changes to the highest grades. But beyond that, he had autonomy to work on behalf of the Illuminati as he saw fit.

Marchese di Costanzo was given the task of writing to the Royal York (one of the administrative centers for the Lodges in the area) and politely mention that there was something of a discrepancy between the fees that were offered to the Grand Lodge by the Illuminati's Lodge Theodore and the services and benefits they received in return. By this point, Lodge Theodore had become a profitable venture for the Royal York, who noticed the large increase in subscription fees that had come from the Illuminati's cover venture. Not wanting to lose out on this money, the Royal York proposed a solution. In return for the continued subscriptions, the Lodge Theodore would receive more access to the great secrets of the Freemasons. Should the Illuminati send a representative up to Berlin, he would be able to learn these secrets in person. Costanzo himself was again chosen by Knigge to make the journey. He set off during April of 1780, hoping to reach Prussia in fairly quickly. Once there, he was to be given the secret instruction that he was to find some way of lowering the amount the Illuminati were paying to the Freemasons. But Costanzo was delayed en route, having gotten into a heated argument with a Frenchman he had encountered in his carriage. The two had fallen out over a lady who happened to be travelling with them, so much so that the Frenchman took the time to send a message ahead to the carriage's destination, Berlin. It warned the King that Costanzo was in fact a spy. The message was enough that Costanzo was immediately locked away upon entering Berlin. He was only released when the Grand Master of the Freemason's Grand York personally intervened. But there was nothing the man could do to prevent Costanzo from being banished, and the Illuminati man was sent back to the Areopagus without having accomplished anything at all. It was just one of the difficulties that Knigge would have to deal with.

One of the major issues that Knigge faced came from the Areopagus's efforts to insert the Illuminati into the more legitimate Freemasonry as an official branch of the organization. The Illuminati already controlled Lodge Theodore, though it found itself lacking in local power thanks to a nearby Lodge that pulled rank. The complicated system of Freemason autonomy meant that – while the Illuminati held much control over their own Lodge – they found themselves having to bow to the nearby Elect Masters. There had been efforts to similarly infiltrate this group, but only one Illuminati member had succeeded. This meant that – for now – there was no way of transforming the Lodge Theodore into an official combination of the Illuminati and the Freemasons. By the end of January, 1781, Knigge had managed to convince members of the Masters Elect to increase the power of the Lodge Theodore, to the point where the Illuminati could create smaller Lodges in their own image. But true independence was in no way, shape, or form about to be discussed. Never mind giant global conspiracies; the Illuminati were struggling to control the secret societies in a small region of Bavaria.

That the organization was so quickly lost and at a crossroads can be a good demonstration of how difficult it can be to entirely take over the world. If we're to believe the conspiracy theories, the global Illuminati network has long been pulling the strings behind every major event for the past two centuries. But that this stage of their existence, barely five years from being a thought in Weishaupt's mind, the Illuminati found themselves falling prey to internal struggles and squabbles. This is important as it reveals the very nature of the organization and why the idea of prolonged, hidden, and effective power is inherently flawed. At their heart – whether that meant Weishaupt, Knigge, or the Areopagus – there was no agreement. Opinions pulled in every direction. This very human quality – to entertain one's own opinions – means that sustained power of the sort described in the conspiracy theories is incredibly unlikely. As we will see in the coming chapters, managing to maintain control and direction for the Illuminati in just a few years can be almost beyond possible. So how was Knigge set to handle this existential threat to the Illuminati?

Knigge quickly realized that – if he was to have any success in extracting a better deal from the Freemasons – he would have to go to a higher power. However, this was always going to be difficult. Knigge was aware that any communications or any petitions to Lodges in London and other far-flung countries would always have been too obvious. Any attempt to gain autonomy in the form of a constitution would quickly become obvious that the Illuminati were working towards their own independence. Far from controlling the world, there was little the Illuminati could do to control local Masonic Lodges. Until this was possible, they would have to slow down their plans for expansion.

While the plans for expansion were slowed down, Knigge turned his attentions inwards. Having cooled the heated relationship between Weishaupt and the Areopagus, he began to focus on the other aspects of his tasks. This included revising the structure of the Illuminati. As it was, they controlled three Masonic Lodges, and Knigge decided that following the structure of the Freemasons remained the best option. By 1782, on the 20th of January, he put forward his new grade system. Once this was approved, the Illuminati would be structure along three distinct classes. These were:

Class I – The Nursey
This would be the first order that people entered into and would contain the Noviciate, the Minerval, and the Illuminatus Minor.

Class II – The Masonic Grades
These were borrowed wholesale from the Freemasons, though they were titled there as Apprentice, Companion, and Master. After these members could advance to a second tier within Class II, which included the Scottish Novice and the Scottish King. Class II clearly took influence directly from the Masons.

Class III – The Mysteries
The upper echelon of Illuminati membership, these were separated into the lesser mysteries, order that were titled Priest and Prince, and the greater mysteries, which were titled Mage and King. So difficult was it to enter into these higher positions that it was unlikely that the rituals or ceremonies for these tiers were ever even written down.

Having laid out a new structure for the group, Knigge began to reform the Illuminati along his own views. Having grown disillusioned with the Freemasons for not ascribing to his own ideals, here was a chance to reshape the Illuminati only a few years after they had come into existence. Far from a global order, they were still very much a local concern. Knigge, however, hoped to change that. As ever, the solution lay in recruitment.

Whereas the Illuminati recruitment had been something of an experimental system up to this point, Knigge decided to take a much more deliberate approach. This time, aware of the difficulties he faced from the Freemasonry upper levels, he decided that he would target men already in positions of power. Whereas Weishaupt had favored impressionable students who he could mold in his image, Knigge wanted men of power and influence, especially those who were already wardens or masters within existing Lodges. Once such people were recruited, it would place the entire administrative capability of the Lodge under Illuminati control. Baron de Witte, who was master of the Constancy Lodge in Aachen, was one such recruit. After he was brought into the fold by Knigge, he succeeded in turning every Freemason in his Lodge into an Illuminati member. This change in strategy brought with it a rapid expansion, far quicker and of greater quality than in the preceding years. After only a short time, it seemed as though Knigge and his tactics were working. By the spring of 1782, the Illuminati found they had a foothold in Austrian Lodges, with their numbers totaling around 300. Unlike the original recruits, only 20 or so of the new wave were actually students.

Around this time, Weishaupt noticed that not all of the people in Lodge Theodore were entirely on board with the Illuminati's presence. Those who had been Freemasons before the Illuminati had arrived or had joined under the guise of Freemasonry were beginning to grumble. Weishaupt, sticking to his principles despising despotism, offered the Lodge a deal. He would willingly split the Lodge in two and allow those who wanted nothing to do with the Illuminati to go their own way. Somewhat unexpectedly, few people took him up on the offer and, quite quickly, Lodge Theodore was entirely under the control of Weishaupt and the Illuminati.

Now that they had the full backing of their Lodge, a growing influence, and greater numbers, the Illuminati felt justified in trying to exert their power. The Order wrote to the Royal York and informed the Freemason authorities that Lodge Theodore intended to "sever relations" with headquarters. As a means of justifying their actions, the Illuminati listed their consistent and dutiful paying of fees, for which they had not received greater insight into the Masonic world, for which their own member (Costanzo) had been poorly treated, and a general inability by the Royal York to provide support. Lodge Theodore, they declared, was now to be considered entirely independent and entirely autonomous.

At the time, the Freemasons themselves facing a great deal of internal turmoil. Having existed for far longer than the Illuminati, they had themselves succumb to many of the same problems. Schisms and internal disagreements had led to the establishing of many different branches and interpretations of Freemasonry. Just as with the Illuminati, the Freemasons found themselves squabbling and unable to move forward. Unlike the Illuminati, this was complicated by the fact that the Freemasons were an international organization. Prince Carl of Södermanland, for example, was ostensibly the leader of the Rite of Strict Observance. But he had been accused of attempting to bring the Rite into the fold of the

Swedish Rite, to the annoyance of many members. The German Lodges began to look elsewhere and depended on Duke Ferdinand (who was in charge of Brunswick-Wolfenbüttel) for guidance. Duke Ferdinand disagreed with Prince Carl, while many of the Freemasons disagreed with everyone else. In the background, somewhat quietly, the Illuminati were happy that the attentions were being diverted elsewhere. It allowed them the opportunity to solidify their power base. While the Freemasons began to focus on what would become the Convent of Wilhelmsbad, the Illuminati, led by Knigge and Weishaupt, were overseeing increasing successes.

But therein lay the problem with suggesting that the Illuminati were in any way a global concern, or that their influence today depends on an 18th Century domination of political thought. Instead, the organization was only able to control a small region in Germany and nearby. Rather than influencing all of Europe, their rise was marked by the very same problems that befell the Freemasons. Arguments, disagreements, and human nature. As we will see in the next chapter, they would have to put these aside if they were to take advantage of an amazing opportunity.

The Illuminati Were Just Lucky

Not all of the stories about the Illuminati position them as a clandestine society behind every major event of the past three centuries. In some versions of their history, they have been described as being simply lucky. They chanced into an opportune moment, or so the story goes. In order to remain both fair and impartial, efforts should be made to look at every side of an argument. If we are quick to disprove that the Illuminati were one of the world's most secretly powerful organizations, we should just as easily be able to prove that this was still a society built by intelligent men with very firm ideas about how they were able to change the world. So, were the Illuminati just lucky, or were they able to make some very intelligent moves towards reorganizing the world in their own image? As ever, the truth lies somewhere between the two positions.

It is certainly true that the Illuminati benefitted from timing. At a critical juncture in their history, when they were hoping to expand and recruit a greater number of more influential people, their chief rivals happened to be going through something of a crisis. As it stood, the divisions and arguments that had surfaced within the Freemasons meant that the Illuminati were presented with an excellent opportunity to take advantage of the chaos for their own benefit. In terms of providing the Illuminati with an opportunity, few moments seemed as opportune as the Convent of Wilhelmsbad. The very same Lodge that Weishaupt had joined some years previous was now seemingly tearing itself apart. The schisms that emerged within the Rite of the Strict Observance threatened to destroy Freemasonry in

Bavaria and beyond. But what exactly were they arguing about?

The matter was somewhat complicated, but it came to a head in the early 1780s. Having been originally planned for late 1781, the Wilhelmsbad Convent was reorganized for July of 1782. It would prove to be the last meeting of the Strict Observance as people knew it. Organized in the spa town of Wilhelmsbad, the Convent was organized to determine the future of the Strict Observance, and thus the future of the biggest and most influential Masonic Lodge in the region. In simple terms, there were two sides to the argument. On one side were those who favored the German approach to Freemasonry that emphasized the Germanic and mystical elements of the Masons. This group was led by Duke Ferdinand and Prince Charles. On the other side of the argument were the Martinists, a branch of Christian esoteric mysticism that focused on the fall from grace of mankind and how the species could be reintegrated into this divine knowledge. Both sides claimed to hold sway over the Freemason's Lodges in the region, with their chief disagreements concerning the ritualistic elements of the Masons. Both sides differed on how they felt the ceremonies and rituals should be organized, how they should be conducted, and which one was right. The Martinists were led by Jean-Baptiste Willermoz. The two sides disagreed over which route the Strict Observance should take.

But it should also be noted that there were certain voices at the gathering that did not agree with either side. Johann Joachim Christoph Bode was one such high ranking Mason, who seemed to be appalled by the prospect of the Martinists and openly offered his dissent towards the mystical aspects of the higher grades of the Freemasons. The real problem for Bode was that he did not have an alternative solution to promote. Also opposed to both main sides was Franz Dietrich von Ditfurth, the Master of a Lodge in Wetzlar named the Joseph of the Three Helmets Lodge. Ditfurth was also a judge, a respected and influential member of his local community. He was also a member of the Illuminati. Acting as something of a representative for the Order, he made his voice heard in public, calling for a back to basics approach. Freemasonry should, he claimed, return to the three basic degrees of Novice, Journeyman, and Master. All of the mystical elements distracted from the work of the Freemasons. Despite the respect many held for Ditfurth, the sheer numbers on the other sides meant that his proposal was the least likely to be decided upon. As it stood, both mystical sides of the argument held their own plans for reforming the upper grades of Freemasonry, but neither could honestly claim that they were clear and well thought out. Everyone knew they wanted change, but had very little idea of what that change should be.

This was ideal for the Illuminati. As luck would have it, the divisions between the Masons opened up in front of them and allowed the Order to fill the void, presenting themselves as a credible alternative. Ditfurth was the chief representative at the meetings, though he was ably assisted by Knigge, who was working behind the scenes. Knigge had been given total autonomy by the Illuminati leaders to act on their behalf, and he had come up with a plan. The first option he suggested had been to try to broker an alliance between all sides, with the Illuminati acting as the peacemakers. This would, it was thought, increase trust in Knigge, Weishaupt, and the rest of the Illuminati and provide them with a greater platform of power. Weishaupt was quick to dash this theory, however, seeing little profitability in being allied to what he saw as a dying institution. Seeing the Illuminati as the future, he and Knigge developed a plan whereby they would kindle the divisions between the Freemasons and then recruit those members whom they liked best, being as they appeared the only credible party. This would allow the Illuminati to turn the Freemasons' divisions to their own advantage, swelling their ranks with the best and brightest while ensuring an influential and powerful crop of new recruits to act out Illuminati policies.

The plan was put into action by Ditfurth, acting on the behalf of the others. As Willermoz put forward ideas for the Martinists, and Prince Charles attempted to explain the German mystics' proposals, Ditfurth made moves to block their actions. Such proposals could not be put into action, he argued, without the full details of the ceremonies and rituals being revealed to every single delegate. How else could they vote fairly without knowing what they were voting for? As it stood, both the German mystics and the Martinists wanted to institute new rituals, imbued with what they considered to be ancient knowledge. But these rituals were only to be learned once a member reached a high enough rank. The delegates in attendance were not at such a rank and could therefore not be permitted to see either of the proposals for higher grades. The frustration on both sides was clear, but Ditfurth had easily convinced the delegates, prompted by Knigge's maneuvering.

Such was the annoyance on behalf of the German mystics that they showed the first signs of being willing to compromise. The Illuminati – through Ditfurth – had finally put together an alternative solution. All of the highest grades would simply be scrapped. What had descended into a complex mix of rites and ceremonies would be abandoned, and the highest tier would simply be a fourth level, one which promised no revelations of ancient knowledge and no source of mystical power. The German mystics could see that this was far from what was being proposed and could identify the Illuminati as an increasingly credible threat. They put forward Count Kollowrat from their ranks to join up to the new Order, planting someone in the Illuminati ranks who might be able to nurture an alliance in the coming times.

But despite Ditfurth's efforts to promote the Illuminati as a credible alternative, his proposals fell on deaf ears. There was a clear intention at the Covenant of Wilhelmsbad to clarify the mess that the higher ranks of the Freemasons had become, but the Illuminati's solution went too far. Though it was simple and easy to understand, many felt that the esoteric mysticism was an essential part of the Freemasons' rituals and could not be so easily abandoned. Ditfurth was quick to notice his failure to convince many people. He left the venue ahead of schedule and dispatched a note to the Areopagus informing them of his failure. Nothing good, he wrote, could be expected to come of the gathering.

Though it appeared on the surface as though the illuminati had failed, the real aftermath of the events at Wilhelmsbad were yet to be understood. The Convent had been intended to repair the schisms that had appeared in the Freemasons at this time. But, with everyone so keen to leave everyone satisfied, the gathering had instead had the opposite effect. No one got what they wanted. There were minor administrative changes made to the higher grades of membership, though little in effect actually changed. Those who had been in charge at the start of the assembly remained in power, meaning that all of the political maneuvering and conniving was very much still apparent. The same power struggle for dominance within the Bavarian Freemasons remained in place, with each and every Lodge increasingly convinced of both their own independence and their own superiority. This was likely realized, as there was a concerted effort at the end of the assembly to try and make it look as though changes had been made. A great deal of noise was made regarding the numbering of the Lodges, changes in etiquette, and the titles applied to certain positions. Though these could be held up as products of the Convent, they actually made little difference and did nothing to repair the damage that had been apparent at the start of the meetings.

So even while Ditfurth had believed himself to have lost, he and the Illuminati benefitted from the fact that no one else won. So little progress was made that the Illuminati were able to stand by and watch as the Strict Observance did nothing to save itself from inevitable collapse. The Strict Observance made a number of key errors. They denounced and disowned their own origin myth, as well as reorganizing the higher grades. This latter change meant that their highest ranking members before the alterations were now no longer bound to the Strict Observance. While the group had been defined by (and had very much benefitted from) the strict control that gave them their title, this was now seemingly abandoned, and the process of power devolution undermined the central authority of the group. Many of the additions to the rules and rituals were enough to appall certain members, with people such as Bode being horrified by the addition of Martinist principles. Almost immediately, Bode began talks with Knigge and was a fully-fledged member of the Illuminati by January of 1783. Just a month later, Charles of Hesse had been recruited in a similar fashion.

Without really doing anything, the Illuminati had strengthened themselves. Their biggest rival and the blockage to their unfettered recruitment was steadily imploding and seemingly unable to stop it. Rather than benefitting from any single genius move or some great masterstroke from Knigge, the Illuminati were fortunate that their rivals were so shortsighted. However, they must be given some credit for positioning themselves into a place where they benefited from such an implosion. More opportunistic than Machiavellian, but more orchestrated than blind luck, there was a fine balance to the politicking of the Illuminati. And it was not yet finished, as the Illuminati still had one or two tricks up their sleeve.

Even though Knigge's attempts at making an alliance with many of the other German Lodges had failed, the Illuminati did not give up. These were the perfect recruiting grounds, and being able to share resources with other Masonic Lodges would be a huge boost to their ambitions. It fell on Weishaupt to take over the process. Though Knigge was by this point the driving force behind many of the Illuminati's actions, Weishaupt still played an important role in the organization. After all, he had founded the entire Order. In the aftermath of the Convent of Wilhelmsbad, he proposed a different alliance for the German Lodges, one which neatly sidestepped the divisive issue. Under Weishaupt's proposal, the Lodges would be allied together in a kind of federation. Inside the federation, every Lodge would practice a uniform, agreed-upon system across the first three (traditional) degrees of Freemasonry. Once members reached the next tiers, it would be down to the individual Lodges as to how they would proceed. In addition to this, a member of any of the allied Lodges could pay a visit to any other Lodge within the federation. Every Lodge master within the alliance was to be promoted via an election, with no subscription fees to be paid at all to any central authority (though Lodges could still charge local fees). To oversee good behavior, there would be a representative council called the Scottish Directorate that would be formed of people from many difference Lodges. This council would be able to settle any disputes, check any finances, and even authorize the founding of new Lodges. In addition to these changes, there were many other slight alterations to the structure and oversight of the Freemasons.

As it stood, Weishaupt's proposed alliance was designed to alter an issue which many people had with the Freemasons in Germany, in that the ideals the groups supposedly believed in seemed to clash with the organization's practice. Any ideas of equality (a Masonic principle) were seemingly forgotten once members moved past the three traditional ranks. Those in the higher degrees were often only able to pursue their interests and continue along the Masonic path based on their resources. Should a Mason hope to practice alchemy or mysticism, then they would need money to do so. Only by conducting these studies could the Freemasons hope to move into the fourth degrees. To men like Knigge and Weishaupt, this seemed to be a major issue and one which would be combated by the alliance. But the two men had an alternative intention. As well as solving a seeming crisis within the Freemasons, it would provide the Illuminati with a brilliant recruiting platform. They would be able to spread their Order throughout the ranks of German Freemasonry. It was not long before the edict was agreed upon and circulated around the various Masonic halls. Few people knew of the alliance's true intentions.

Even the announcement that was sent around the Lodges was carefully planned by the Illuminati. The document outlined the faults inherent in the current system, chief among which related to whom the Freemasons were recruiting. As the circular mentioned, many of those people who were admitted into the Freemasons were actually ill-suited to the organization and were only really present thanks to their wealth. This, they felt, was a corruption that was also prone to occur in the wider society. It proved convincing, and soon enough, Weishaupt's proposals were being put into practice.

Having helped draft the changes, the Illuminati themselves were among the first to make changes to their structure. Lodge Theodore – still their headquarters – began to change. As the regulations applied to many of the higher grades of Freemasonry were removed, and each Lodge began to construct their own fourth degrees, the Illuminati followed suit. Establishing themselves as the Grand Lodge in their province, the Illuminati (with Knigge acting on their behalf) wrote a letter that accused the Royal York of decadence. To drive the point home, the Illuminati turned towards one of their old enemies.

They accused the Royal York of colluding with and being corrupted by the Jesuits. Strict Observance (or what was left of it) suffered from similar accusations, with the Illuminati claiming that the group was "devoid of all moral virtue." Elsewhere, they accused certain rites of being in league with the Swedes, positioning the Illuminati and their Lodge Theodore as the only true bastion of legitimate Freemasonry. The Illuminati had seen their chance open up before them and they had taken it.

Or so it had seemed. What they had thought to be a devastating number of accusations proved to have the opposite effect. Weishaupt, rather than turning many Freemasons to his cause, had managed to alienate, annoy, and offend many members. The plan of infiltrating the Freemasons and co-opting their members seemed fundamentally flawed. Other Freemasons such as the Grand Lodge of the Grand Orient of Warsaw (who ran the Freemasons in Lithuania and Poland) might have been interested, but they demanded independence in light of these accusations. They, like many others, were suspicious of the Illuminati's intentions. With many Lodges happy to participate in the first three degrees of Freemasonry, the Illuminati had trouble convincing others of the benefits of joining them in the higher ranks. This was where the true power lay, and other Lodges were happy to keep it for themselves. Nevertheless, the Illuminati had some success. By the beginning of 1783, they had managed to gain full control of seven Masonic Lodges.

It was not that surprising that the attempts of Weishaupt and Knigge were met with relative failure. Though the Lodge Theodore was growing in size, it was still very much a new arrival on the block. Many other Freemason

Lodges were much older and thus commanded much more respect. Though the Illuminati had proved lucky in some areas and had managed to capitalize on that, they were guilty of overreaching and attempting to move too far ahead of their means. It was a clumsy approach, one that reflected a lack of awareness of the sentiment towards their Lodge among the Freemasons. What luck they had experienced, they were almost as quick to squander. Furthermore, it helped to ostracize the very members whom the Illuminati wanted to recruit. At this time, they were still very much symbiotically attached to the Freemasons. Not yet strong enough to stand on their own feet, they depended on the older organization as a means of legitimizing themselves in the eyes of potential recruits. Ostensibly, to the outward eye, they were just another Lodge. The truth of the Illuminati was not yet public knowledge. Accordingly, those Freemasons who might agree with the Illuminati's distrust of mysticism and those who did not like the Martinists might be ideal recruits. But they were people who were very much invested in their own independence, something they did not want to give up to the Illuminati. A good example of this was Ditfurth, who despite representing the Illuminati at the Convent of Wilhelmsbad, had been keen to pursue his own agenda and quick to give up.

Ditfurth's own allegiance was quickly removed once he found something more suited to his principles, revealing the difficulty the Illuminati faced. Following the formation of the alliance, there began to emerge a second gathering of Lodges, this time it would be a gather that grouped together the non-mystical Lodges that were around Frankfurt. It was named the Eclectic Alliance and seemed to be ideologically in line with exactly the kind of group the Illuminati was striving toward. The only problem was that it was not their idea. However, the lucky emergence of this Eclectic Alliance provided the opportunity to steady the ship, and after a short discussion, the Illuminati agreed that their Lodges should join. Furthermore, they were welcomed to take seats on the committee and help to draft the statutes and rules for the alliance. They were lucky enough to be trusted with this amount of influence and responsibility, though there seemed to be little tactical advantage that came from the alliance. The agreement did not provide them with that much access to new recruits. In fact, when men such as Ditfurth noticed that the other Lodges in the Eclectic Alliance were more ideologically in line with his own philosophies, he began to distance himself from the Illuminati. He was not alone. Indeed, so successful was the Eclectic Alliance over the Illuminati's federation – and so little control did they have over the group – that it can actually be considered a hindrance to their efforts. All of the subtle planning they had made when trying to place themselves in an opportune moment seemed to be undone.

But the alliance did have one benefit: it kept them in the game. The real luck of the Illuminati seems to have been that they were consistently able to avoid irrelevancy. Time and time again, they hit issues in their plans. Either they were not trusted enough, or they made mistakes, or events did not go as planned. But every time, the group managed to pull through by cleverly seizing on the opportunities that presented themselves. The traditional view of the Illuminati seems to have them pulling the strings behind the world stage, subtly manipulating global events. But in the 18th Century, they struggled to keep a hold of the Freemasons in Bavaria and the surrounding areas. They were lucky enough to be consistently presented with opportunities to redeem themselves and to stay in the game, though were often clever enough to jump on these opportunities in the perfect manner. It was a delicate balancing act between luck, failure, success, and opportunism. From it all, the Illuminati were steadily becoming more powerful and more influential. As we will see in the next chapter, they were about to get a lot closer to achieving their goals.

The Illuminati Changed the World

Throughout this book, our discussions of the Illuminati have been limited to a small geographical area and have barely covered a decade. In terms of European history, this is only a tiny window into the continent's storied past. Indeed, we have spent much time looking in detail at the Freemasons, another society altogether. Now that we are roughly at the halfway point of the book, you might find yourself asking just how such a famous society was so confined to a brief moment in time. We made a promise at the beginning of this book to examine the facts. There are many myths and legends that exist about the Order, but there can be no doubting their existence. We know what we know because of evidence, the documents (often written by the men named in this book) that have been passed down to our modern age and provide us with definitive evidence of their existence. The Illuminati existed, but how exactly did such a seemingly small group manage to change the world? To answer this question, we should examine the society when they were at their administrative peak.

In the previous chapter, we witnessed the problems that the Illuminati were facing. To expand as a secret society and to put their ideas into practice – to have a demonstrable effect on the world – they would need to grow. In order to grow, they would need to recruit. They had decided that the Freemasons gave them a potential pool of talent, and they had worked to ingratiate themselves into the competing organization, seemingly hoping to take it apart from the inside. But due to poor judgement and poor luck, this had not come to pass. Despite their lofty ambitions, the Illuminati had not quite reached the heights they had strived to attain. But that is not to say that they were not succeeding.

When we look at the recruitment of the Illuminati on a small scale – on a person-to-person basis – it seems clear that they were actually moderately successful. They might have planned to raid the Freemasons for the very best and brightest, displacing the centuries-old society as the dominant clandestine organization, but that was always something of an unrealistic dream. Instead, their individual level recruitment had provided them with a steadily growing list of members. Not only was the membership growing, but the men coming into the group were of a high quality. People seemed to be keen to believe in the principles laid out by the Illuminati, and it seemed that there was certainly something appealing about how they envisaged the world.

All around them, Bavaria was changing. In the short time since the Illuminati had formed, the ruling party of the country had changed. Charles Theodore – the man who lent his name to the Illuminati's Masonic Lodge – had ascended to power. Charles Theodore had been the man who had originally outlawed secret societies, but his increasing amounts of power had steadily led to a growing liberalism in the region. This was not appreciated by everyone. Though a longstanding ruler of a number of territories, Theodore was not strong-willed enough to drive his ideas forward. Those whose positions seemed to be threatened by a liberalization of the country – members of the court and the clergy – managed to cajole and convince the ruler to reverse his stance. What had seemed like an age of acceptance of liberal ideas was quickly turned around into quite the opposite. Amid growing societal discord, Charles

Theodore allowed his powerful and privileged advisors to guard their own positions, at the expense of the region's more progressive thinkers. Across Bavaria, a brief moment of accepted liberalism was dashed by a renewed clamp down on such ideas.

Such a move seemed ideal for the Illuminati. They were founded on the very ideas that Theodore was attempting to repress. Though their Lodge might have been named for the man, the principles of the Illuminati who operated under the guise of Freemasons could not have been further from the ruler's own. Across Bavaria, people were beginning to resent Charles Theodore more and more, especially among the educated (though not necessarily overly-privileged) classes. The situation was ideal for a seemingly enlightened secret society who wanted to recruit new members. With the stated aim of changing the world, the Illuminati began to escalate their recruitment programs.

First to be brought into the group were a number of disaffected Freemasons who had found the growing Martinist influence on the Prudence Lodge to be distasteful. They found in the Lodge Theodore a group who were not nearly as invested in the more esoteric aspects of the Freemason experience and instead focused their attentions on contemporary philosophies and the ideas that were being deemed unlawful by the ruling government. As groups such as this defected to the Illuminati, the Areopagus and Weishaupt realized that they would need somewhere to house their efforts. They chose a mansion of their own, one surrounded by high walls and lush gardens, and one with a library that they could fill with the kind of liberal literature that drove their ideology.

The same kind of expansion was happening across Germany. In many different regions, local Illuminati strongholds were beginning to emerge. Though small at first, they represented a spreading influence that moved across the country in reaction to changing government policies and dissatisfaction with both the ruling elite and the practices of the Freemasons. Attitudes were changing across the region, and the Illuminati had come to represent that change. Numbers were still relatively low, but they were growing well. The circle found in Mainz, for example, had seen its numbers almost double in a short space of time. Where there had previously been around 30 members, there were now 61. The state's views on Catholicism and stated anti-liberal stances only fueled the fire. Similar growth was found in parts of Austria, as well as new branches of the group springing up in places such as Warsaw and Bratislava, and as far away as Milan, Tyrol, and Switzerland. The Illuminati were quickly becoming a European concern, rather than simply a Bavarian group.

By the end of 1784, this seemed to have hit unprecedented heights. Weishaupt, despite his efforts, could not have expected to see the membership grow so smoothly. The accounts and records kept by the group at the time show as many as 650 official members, though the communications and private accounts by Weishaupt and others point towards there having been potentially 2,500 Illuminati members during this period. It is likely that the men were counting the other Freemasons who were members of the Lodges under Illuminati control (though not actual members at that time), but there is little reason to suspect that the real number did not lie somewhere between the two estimates. For a group that was started in a secretive university meeting, the growth in under a decade was astonishing. It was less about the hard numbers and more to do with the geographical spread of the influence. Twenty powerful and influential members in Milan, for example, were a very valuable resource for a group who saw themselves as a potentially internationally dominant organization. In order to change the world, this level of influence was more important than simple raw numbers.

This was perhaps due to one of the key changes that Knigge and the Areopagus had implemented. While Weishaupt had been content to focus on students and young men, there was a conscious decision to focus on the more influential recruits. This meant that the newest members were typically lawyers, doctors, men of the church, academics, and other professional peoples. These were far more valuable to the organization than students and men of little influence. But even more important were those who could wield true power. Men such as Karl August and Ernest II were both members, as were the Grand Duke of Saxe-Weimar-Eisenach and the Duke of Saxe-Gotha-Altenburg respectively. Ernest's brother (and the man who would eventually succeed him) August had joined, as had Karl von Dalberg (the governor of Erfurt) and Duke Ferdinand of Brunswick-Wolfenbüttel. Duke Ferdinand brought with him Johann Friedrich von Schwarz from his Masonic connections. Count Metternich of Koblenz was also a member. In all these were people with legitimate legislative power, people who could affect real change in the world. In the Illuminati, they happened to see something of real value.

There were even successes in other areas of Europe, recruiting quite influential figures for what was still a relatively small society when considered on the wider international stage. For example, in Vienna, the Illuminati managed to recruit the following people:

- The governor of Galicia (Count Brigido)
- The chancellor of Bohemia (Count Leopold Kolowrat)
- The vice-chancellor of Bohemia (Baron Kressel)
- The chancellor of Hungary (Count Pálffy von Erdöd)
- The governor of Transylvania (and also Grand Master of the local Lodge, Count Banffy)
- The ambassador to London (Count Stadion)
- And the minister of public education (Baron von Swieten)

Even outside of their native regions, the Illuminati were succeeding in recruiting people of real power, those who could not only influence lawmakers and courts, but also those who could further the recruitment. With such an illustrious list of people on their books, it is easy to see why so many ensuing generations have been willing to believe that the Illuminati control vast swathes of legislative power. For a brief period in the 18th Century, they had a very real influence on the part of Central Europe where they were based. Thanks to the works of Knigge, Weishaupt, and many others, there had been a series of real successes in the world of recruitment.

But the Illuminati were not always successful. Despite their laudable attempts to recruit people of real power, they were also marked by a number of notable failures. One of the most famous was their attempt to bring Johann Kaspar Lavater into the fold. Lavater was Swiss, famous for his works in theology and poetry. A well-respected individual, he seemed an ideal fit for the organization and exactly the kind of man they hoped to recruit. But when Knigge offered membership to Lavater, it was summarily rejected. According to the Swiss poet, the Illuminati's stated aims – those of rationalist and humanist principles being enacted in governments across Europe – was not something that could be achieved by a secret society. Not believing in their methods, he declined the invitation. Not only that, but the failure left a lasting impact on Lavater. He let it be known that, in his opinion, such a concerted recruitment drive would eventually be the undoing of the society. As the Illuminati sought out increasingly powerful and influential recruits, the poet believed that this would cause them to forget the ideals and goals that had first inspired them.

Lavater was not alone. Christoph Friedrich Nicolai went further in his investigations into what the Illuminati had to offer. A writer from Berlin, he was another person who seemed to be ideally suited to the ideas the Order were trying to promote. He went as far as to join up, but it was not long before he became less than convinced by the Order's capabilities. Discussing why he eventually grew disillusioned with the group, he described their aims as "chimeric" and believed that the group were using similar tactics to those used by the Illuminati's old enemies, the Jesuits, something that he believed was dangerous. Though he technically remained a member, he was not very active and was one of the few dissenting voices we have from that time. Not willing to recruit other members and critical of the group's methods, Nicolai was a good indication that not everyone was so seduced by the Illuminati's approach.

At the start of this chapter, we set out to investigate whether the Illuminati managed to change the world. It is one of the most enduring claims levelled against them, though often it relates to an entirely different interpretation of the Illuminati. What we have just seen, the period of history that we have covered, relates to the high water mark of the Illuminati's influence. During this time, they managed to recruit a number of very influential people. They had members in Great Britain, Italy, Switzerland, Germany, Austria, and other countries. Not only that, but these were people of real importance. For a society that had been formed less than ten years earlier, this is certainly impressive.

But as we will see in coming chapters, the Illuminati did not manage to turn this success in recruiting into palpable, real-world change. We know that they had a defined ideology, one that promoted the ideas of the Enlightenment and hoped to add a degree of rationalism to governance. But they struggled to even make this change in their local government. They were successful at the time because Bavaria was the exact opposite of what they wanted. Repressive, reactionary, and all too keen to clamp down on liberal ideas, the Illuminati's home playing field was never really affected by their presence. While they did well to recruit important people, they failed to convert that recruitment success into real results. However, though the Illuminati did not manage to affect any real change in 18th Century politics, they certainly left a legacy. As we will see in the next chapter and beyond, however, that legacy was not always entirely positive.

The Illuminati: Satanism, Witchcraft, Rosicrucianism, and the Occult

It might not be a surprise to learn that the Illuminati were not the only secret society competing in 18th Century Europe. We have already encountered the Freemasons and their centuries-old society, one that was known across the continent. But there were other groups as well, similarly outlawed and perceived as being just as dangerous as the Illuminati. When discussing the schism within the Freemasons, we briefly mentioned the rituals and ceremonies that were used by the Masons. While many saw these as simple traditions – and some went as far as to admit that they were invented for the purpose – other secret societies focused far more heavily on the magic, the occult, and the mystical. While the Illuminati were founded on rationalist, seemingly scientific principles, there were other orders that were not nearly as modern. In our modern age, many people have conflated the efforts of such societies with the Illuminati. As such, Weishaupt's order has been accused of everything from Satanism to witchcraft. But were they really involved in such practices? And how did they come to be tarred with the reputation of other secret societies?

While we have been using the phrase "secret society" throughout this book, it has quickly become clear that there were few secrets that were that well-kept in 18th Century Europe. The entire premise of organizations such as the Freemasons and the Illuminati relied upon revealing the secret to others in order to recruit them. This created a strange balance between secrecy and publicity. In essence, many people knew that these groups existed, even if they did not entirely understand them. But alongside the two most famous examples, there was a third major secret society, one which we have not mentioned up until this point. The Rosicrucians, in many ways, seemed to be the antithesis of everything the Illuminati stood for. It was only natural that the two should come into conflict at some stage.

Before we go any further, we should pause to take a moment to learn more about Rosicrucianism. As you might have guessed, the Rosicrucians were a secret society, also founded in Germany. Dating from the medieval period, they were founded by a man named Christian Rosenkreuz, whose name means – quite literally – "rose cross" and lends the society its title. Like many other secret societies, they claimed to possess "esoteric truths" that had been passed down to them from ancient times. Part of their popularity can be traced to two documents that began to circulate around 17th Century Germany, which presented the Brotherhood of the Rosicrucians as being a laudable Order who hoped to reform mankind. They were opposed to the Roman Catholic religion, in which they were similar to the Illuminati in their quest for a more empirical approach to life. But rather than rationalism, they believed themselves to possess ancient secrets and sciences perfected by Moorish philosophers hundreds of years previous. These seemingly magical and mystical spells and teachings would inform many 18th Century people. They have been named as the place from which Freemasonry borrowed a great deal of ideas for their rituals and ceremonies. This Rosicrucian mysticism, while perhaps not purporting to practice magic as we might understand it today, certainly had a touch of the occult about it. In that respect, they were very much the opposite of the Illuminati's calls for rationalism and modernism.

But the effect of the Rosicrucians on the Freemasons was palpable. Many of their members were intertwined across both orders. It was not uncommon for people to describe themselves as a blend between the two societies. In a similar way to how the Illuminati had infiltrated the Freemasons during the 18th Century, the Rosicrucian Order had managed to do so a century before. By the time Weishaupt first began to think about the Illuminati, the Rosicrucians were already an established presence in the Lodges throughout Germany. Knowing that the two groups would never be able to see eye to eye on many matters, Weishaupt tried very hard to keep the existence of his Illuminati from those who he knew to be Rosicrucians. While the two groups were clearly Protestant in their teachings, the differences ran far deeper. Where the Illuminati were anti-monarchy, the Rosicrucians were in favor of the rule of kings. Where the Illuminati were against the clergy in almost any form, the Rosicrucians believed it had a place in society. Where the Illuminati favored the idea of the Enlightenment-orientated society that was run by people like scientists and philosophers, the Rosicrucians whole-heartedly disagreed.

With two competing secret societies operating within the larger secret society, it was perhaps inevitable that there would be some kind of conflict between the two smaller Orders. One of the factors that proved annoying to various Illuminati members was the Rosicrucian practice of holding séances and other mystical events. These events were described by various members of the Illuminati as being fraudulent, something that seemed to widen the chasm between the two groups. As more and more people became aware of the existence of the Illuminati, it became increasingly more obvious that the two societies would some come into direct conflict.

But that is not to say that the Illuminati did not have members who leaned towards certain elements of mysticism. Perhaps the most famous was Knigge, who had openly admitted to an interest in practices such as alchemy. His knowledge of the occult had meant that he had been the one trusted with drafting the rituals and ceremonies, seemingly the man who was able to give them an authentic flavor. Increasingly, it seemed, a number of Rosicrucians had been joining the Illuminati, the cross-pollination of the two groups a growing trend. As well as Knigge, Kolowrat was actually a member of the Rosicrucian Order, while many of Knigge's direct recruits certainly had mystic sympathies. Prince Charles of Hesse-Kassel was a confirmed mystic and had, on a number of occasions, voiced his distrust of some of the more ardent Illuminati rationalists.

The first blows in the conflict were launched by Johann Christoph von Wöllner, who led the Prussian branch of the Rosicrucians in a sustained and forceful attack against the Illuminati. Wöllner was known to possess a room dedicated to mysticism. He would take doubting patrons inside and, once locked in, convince them of the effectiveness of the magic that the Rosicrucians were said to possess. The room had been specially engineered exactly for this purpose, and though we do not know exactly how, it has been heavily implied that Wöllner used a series of tricks and illusions to convince patrons who would then become members of the Rosicrucian Orders. Using methods such as these, Wöllner and his Order had managed to gain control of one of the most important Masonic Lodges, the Three Globes, as well as those smaller Lodges that served under it. Wöllner used the Three Globes to launch a flurry of accusations at the Illuminati.

Via the mouthpiece of the Rosicrucian controlled Three Globes Grand Lodge, Wöllner and his Order accused the Illuminati of crimes such as atheism (still very much outlawed at the time) and suggested that they were plotting revolutionary activities. This was compounded in April of 1783, when Charles of Hesse was informed by fellow Freemason Frederick the Great that the Lodges in Berlin had come into possession of documents that showed that the Illuminati were to be suspected of atheism, being as the documents contained "appalling materials." Frederick the Great sought to get more information from his Illuminati-aligned friend, asking whether he had ever heard of any such things. To make matters worse, Wöllner and his colleagues spread the word around all of the Berlin Lodges that the Illuminati were not to be trusted, as the group hoped to undermine, corrupt, and do away with all sorts of religion. Preying on the conservative members of the Freemasons, they hoped to ward people off the Illuminati for good. The campaign launched by Wöllner and his Rosicrucians went on throughout the remainder of 1783 and well into 1784. By November of that year, they refused even to accept that any Illuminati member could ever describe himself as a Freemason. It was, in effect, a full scale propaganda campaign.

It was not only limited to Lodges in Berlin. In parts of Austria, the Rosicrucians were launching similar campaigns. They described their Illuminati rivals as being responsible for a string of pamphlets that denounced all sorts of religion. This turned into a surveillance mission, with the Rosicrucians placing Illuminati members such as Joseph von Sonnenfels under constant watch, waiting for the slightest slip-up. Their efforts proved to be successful and even managed to completely close down any form of Illuminati recruitment anywhere in Tyrol.

As well as the campaign from outside the Illuminati, those in the Order found themselves undone by betrayals from within. Throughout the Bavarian Illuminati Lodges, the Rosicrucians had been made aware of many of the group's actions thanks to a well-placed (though never named) informant. This was made even worse when one of the Areopagus – a man named Ferdinand Maria Baader – attempted to join the Rosicrucians. Though his initial attempts seemed to be going well, the Rosicrucians were quickly made aware of Baader's position within the Illuminati. He was told, quite bluntly, that he would not be allowed to join both groups. Baader chose to remain loyal to the Illuminati and wrote the customary resignation letter to the Rosicrucians. In doing so, he boldly claimed that the Rosicrucians possessed no actual mystical knowledge and that they were wrong to ignore those who were "truly illuminated." While they were brash words, he made the mistake of naming the Lodge Theodore, effectively outing it as the headquarters of the Illuminati. It seemed to be a battle that the Rosicrucians were set to win.

But the Illuminati seemed unable to respond. Why, when a band of mystical Rosicrucians appeared to be waging a fierce campaign against the Illuminati, did they appear to be doing so little? The answer is that they were facing some far greater problems that began to originate from within. Having already peaked in terms of their recruiting and their effectiveness, the Illuminati had now begun to embark upon their decline. Choosing to focus inwards, there was little time to respond to the Rosicrucians. But the conflict between the two Orders provides us with an insight into exactly why the Illuminati are viewed as they are today, and why they have so often been accused of witchcraft, Satanism, and all sorts of mysticism.

First, the very existence of the Rosicrucians demonstrates to the modern audience that secret societies that focused on magic and the occult did in fact exist. These were not works of fiction, created to scare and intimidate. While the Rosicrucians may not really have possessed ancient knowledge and magical powers, people certainly believed that they did. Having existed long before the Illuminati, Orders such as the Rosicrucians helped to create the modern conception of what a secret society might be like; secret, mystical, and conducting strange rituals. Though the Illuminati might have been ideologically opposed to the mystics, it is easy to see why so many people are willing to believe they might be capable of such practices. This is especially true when you remember that the Illuminati themselves conducted many of the rituals they lifted wholesale from the Freemasons (which may in turn have been taken from the Rosicrucians). Simply because they became the better known of the two Orders, the Illuminati have since been burdened with the reputation of the Rosicrucians for conducting all sorts of black magic.

So, while the Illuminati were almost definitively against the kind of mysticism and occult that they might be perceived to have conducted, the existence of the Rosicrucians propaganda campaign shows that they were often targeted for misinformation campaigns. As a secret society, it is not entirely possible to simply establish what you are and are not concerned with. As the rumors and salacious lies began to spread among the Freemasons and even the public, the Illuminati were quickly smeared. Unable to fight back, they fell victim to bad publicity that had endured to the modern day. It does not take long to look around the internet and find discussions that link the Illuminati to devil worship, black magic, and various other occult practices. As we have seen, this could hardly have been further from the truth. While members such as Knigge might have dabbled to some extent, the very founding principles of the Illuminati described them as rational, empirical men. That there should still be so many misconceptions demonstrates just how good a campaign the Rosicrucians waged. But as their reputation was sullied, how could the Illuminati not be fighting back? In the next chapter, we will look into the internal conflicts and destructive tendencies that led to the fall of the Illuminati.

The Illuminati are Dead

If we are to believe the modern stories about the Illuminati, they are very much active and very much alive. Still causing trouble around the world in an unending pursuit of global domination, the Illuminati are behind many of the most important world events we have seen in the last centuries. But that tells a very different story from the history books. In the coming chapters, we will begin to see the schism between the Bavarian Illuminati and the modern idea of the Order as it exists today. In doing so, we will have to answer the question: Are the Illuminati dead? If the answer is yes, then what killed them?

In the previous chapter, we saw how difficult the world could become when the Illuminati faced a threat that was as equally adept at moving within the clandestine circles of secret societies. Though Weishaupt and Knigge had done an incredible job in picking up a small group and raising it to the point where they became a serious concern in many parts of Europe, they had not done so without issues. At various points, both men had fallen out with the council of the Illuminati, the so-called Areopagus. As the Illuminati grew increasingly close to the Freemasons, and as they began to grow outside of Bavaria, this council was deemed to be ineffective. Both Knigge and Weishaupt agreed that it could do with a revamp. Rather than empowering the Areopagus, however, they simply replaced it. Instead, there existed the Council of Provincials, who were hampered by the lack of power.

Though they had replaced the Areopagus with an ineffective substitute, the men who had sat on the Areopagus remained as Illuminati members, and they began to make their voices heard. To this point in time, Knigge had acted as the man who healed up relationships between the Areopagus and Weishaupt. But as soon as Knigge left the immediate scene, the two sides would go back to bickering and arguing. Rather than focusing on external threats or progressing the society, they were content to fight amongst themselves. We still have many of Weishaupt's private letters and communications in which he does not hold back in his distaste of many of the Areopagites. These letters were written to those who supposedly trusted, often about those who he supposedly considered his enemies. Such was the collusion within the order, however, that Weishaupt was sometimes wrong in his assumptions. Already, cracks were beginning to appear throughout the structure of the Illuminati.

One of the most serious cracks appeared between Weishaupt and Knigge. Though the two had considerably different principles, they had worked together often for the betterment of the society. Weishaupt, however, had succeeded in driving Knigge further and further away from the center of the group, effectively alienating him within the Illuminati. It was an acknowledged fact that the founder of the Illuminati had been forced to cede a huge amount of control and power to Knigge, and he had never truly forgotten this. Weishaupt wanted his power back. Though Knigge had been trusted as the only man who had been able to construct and create the rituals of the Illuminati – essential to give them the appearance of a credible secret society like the Freemasons – Weishaupt was clearly resentful of what he had lost in the trade. Knigge deserved a huge amount of credit for what he had accomplished, however. Before he had become a member, Weishaupt and his fellow Illuminati (the majority of whom were his students) were limited in their scope and their abilities, if not their ambitions. Once Knigge had been entrusted with the recruitment and the creation of many of the society's internal documents, they had almost instantly begun to grow. Knigge had elevated the Illuminati to the point where a somewhat small and fringe group held an international presence and was considered dangerous enough to be attacked by other, more powerful, secret societies.

For his part, Knigge felt that the hard work he had put into the Illuminati was not being acknowledged. Feeling as though he was underappreciated by the founder of the group, the divisions between the two men's beliefs began to become more of an issue. One of the key issues proved to be Weishaupt's continued stance on clericalism and his absolute abhorrence of the way in which religion was organized and practiced. Knigge perceived this as clashing with his own beliefs in the mystical arts. When Knigge began to recruit more and more people who shared his beliefs – men such as Ditfurth – Weishaupt began to see this as a threat to the founding principles of the Illuminati and an attempt to change the course of the society.

The tension between the two finally erupted during ongoing talks regarding some of Knigge's work. The matter at hand was the grade of Priest, one of the fourth-tier degrees that awaited those who rose through the ranks of the Illuminati. Knigge had been entrusted with writing the materials for the degree and tasked with making them sound suitably mystical so that future members might believe them to be authentic. Not necessarily that they were working, but rather that the new recruits were entering into a centuries-old tradition. Many of the Illuminati of the higher ranks considered the work that Knigge had done to not be his best. It had been described as "florid" by some and "ill-conceived" by others. At its worst, some of the members felt, the ritual made use of "puerile and expensive" regalia. This meant that some of the Illuminati would outright refuse to use Knigge's work, while others only did so after editing it. Things truly became serious when Weishaupt demanded that it be re-written and that Knigge face the critics.

This was not something Knigge wanted to hear. Having already completed the work, he argued that it had been distributed to the Lodges a long time ago. Hence, the people who had heard the rituals had been under the impression that it was ancient. Furthermore, he had done this with Weishaupt's blessing as had been laid out in the original instructions. If the rituals and ceremonies were edited now, then it would appear deeply suspicious and would contravene the blessing Weishaupt had provided some years earlier. Weishaupt did not care. He began to have loud discussions with other Illuminati members about the Priest rituals, describing how they were fundamentally flawed and how Knigge had simply invented it all. Weishaupt was allowing his lack of mystical beliefs to show.

To Knigge, this was deeply insulting. Having heard what Weishaupt was doing, he went straight to the founder and threatened to reveal just how much of the Illuminati's ritual and practice he had simply invented. If everyone found out that it had all been simply concocted by Knigge, then there would be a serious blow to the trust placed in the Illuminati by its recruits. They had all joined up under the impression that the entire thing was genuine, not just the inventions of Knigge. But the two men failed to come to an agreement and tensions between the two continued to simmer and bubble.

As a means of fighting back, Knigge attempted to convene another council, trying to put together a convention of the Areopagites who had provided some counterbalance to Weishaupt's whims. But it proved more difficult to carry out than he had imagined, and the group failed to materialize. It soon became clear that many members of the Areopagus trusted Knigge even less than the founder of the Illuminati with whom he was fighting. As it became clear that he was losing a battle for the hearts and minds of the Illuminati members, Knigge finally bowed out of the fight with Weishaupt and – in July of 1784 – tended his resignation. He left the council by mutual agreement, handing back to them all of the papers and materials that he had used during his time carrying out their wishes. As a response, Weishaupt went out and wrote a retraction, taking back all of the slanders and accusations that he had levelled against Knigge during their falling out. Though it had appeared that he had won the war against Knigge, Weishaupt had only succeeded in robbing the Illuminati of one of its most important members. Much in line with the notion of "cutting off your nose to spite your face," Weishaupt had allowed his petty squabbles to undermine and fracture the Illuminati. Not only had the arguments and disagreements been disruptive, but Knigge's exit meant that the Illuminati had now lost the man who was considered the best recruiter, the best theoretician, and the man who provided them with a bridge to the influence they truly craved. Weishaupt had sounded the death knell of the Illuminati, and he had no idea.

If the differences between Weishaupt and Knigge had signaled the beginning of the end of the Illuminati, then the ripples were felt through every level of the organization. With such clear disputes and differences at the highest levels, it should not have been a surprise to see the lower-ranked Illuminati members taking their cues from those above them. With the Rosicrucians doing their best to damage the Illuminati name, the government increasingly suspicious of liberal-minded secret societies, and the upper echelons arguing among themselves, there was no one around to notice the cracks that were starting to appear in the society.

One of the biggest issues was trying to remain secretive. Though recruitment was essential for the growth of any secret society, there was a decorum and a method behind the attempt to bring additional people in on the secret. The majority of the recruitment – especially as it was handled by Knigge – occurred in smoky rooms, hidden places where people would not be overheard. Furthermore, only those who were considered genuine Illuminati prospects were told about the potential existence of the anti-monarchy, anti-clericalism society. But that was not how many of the lower-ranked Illuminati members were conducting themselves. Despite the secretive nature of their society, there was a great deal of loose talk emanating from many members. This could come in many forms. They might be drunken boasts of secret power made in Bavarian bars, or they might have been a stinging criticism of the monarchy launched in a place where such outlandish principles were never heard. Over dinner parties, Illuminati members hinted about their secret organization's plans to take down the structures of society, to the point where their existence became common knowledge amongst people who had little or nothing to do with secret societies.

Perhaps more worryingly was that these loose lips would often give away the names of those involved. With the principles behind the Illuminati often seeming very threatening against those in power, the protection provided to the group members came in the form of their secret nature. As long as no one knew that you were a member of the radical organization, you were likely safe. But as the information began to leak out of the increasingly loquacious Illuminati members, even this veil of protection was lifted. Soon, the names of the highest ranking members began to circulate among the Bavarian society. For those who held onto powerful and influential government positions, this could be a real problem. As the tide of public opinion was turning against this little understood, clandestine threat, those whose names were linked to the Illuminati (rightly or wrongly) found their positions and their lives coming under growing scrutiny.

By this point in time, Knigge's recruitment tactics had succeeded in filling the Illuminati ranks with people from a wide range of civic and governmental positions. Though Knigge himself had walked away from the group, he left behind a legacy of increased influence. It seemed as though the Illuminati were slowly infiltrating the ranks of government. Though they might not have the people in the highest positions among their number, they were more than stocked with the men who carried out the legislative legwork. Should these men be promoted or rewarded with additional power over time, then the Illuminati would feel their influence grow. Just as they had done with the Freemasons, the plan seemed to be to infiltrate and guide a much larger host body while striving to remain in the shadows.

Indeed, the Illuminati had been so successful at this that there was a period when one's relationship with the Illuminati could have a big influence over interactions with the government. Take, for example, the idea of a legal dispute that might need to be settled in court. With the increased Illuminati presence on the judiciary, you would stand a far greater chance of a favorable result if you were in good standing with the Order. Whether it was judges, lawyers, or simply people who could apply influence, the Illuminati had the members who could provide real assistance in these sort of circumstances, or could deliver real misfortune if their opinion of you was not quite so favorable.

It was this growing level of influence that was gradually noticed by the general populace and steadily resented more and move. The rumors of the Illuminati's powers and influence grew and spread, far exceeding their actual capabilities. While the Order itself was facing major issues on the inside, unable to agree on their direction, the public and the government only saw the looming specter of a very real threat. Unable to see the whole picture, they seemed to vastly overestimate the potential of the Illuminati, adding to the fear and worry that the Order was provoking. Even little things began to get blamed on the Illuminati. When a number of anti-religious leaflets were distributed across Bavaria, the Illuminati were the ones who got the blame. Regardless of whether or not they created the pamphlets (we're not unsure), the fact that so many people were willing to presume this to be true is a key moment in the history of the Illuminati. It marks the moment when they began to take on the role of an urban legend, the unseen bogey man who could be blamed for society's ills. While one version of the Illuminati was busy dying, the other, more modern version was getting ready to rise up in their place.

That is not to say, however, that the public were wrong in their presumptions. While there were clear motivations on behalf of the Illuminati's rivals to discredit and dissolve the Order, these vindictive actions were often based at least partly on some element of the truth. The reason, for example, that so many people were willing to believe that the Illuminati might have distributed the anti-religious pamphlets is because this was perfectly in line with many of the ideas the Illuminati wanted to promote. Even if they had not made the pamphlets themselves, the Illuminati likely did not disagree too strongly with the content. Indeed, such was their influence in the government that it was almost an open secret that the Illuminati's influence in the courts could provide people with preferential treatment. The elected treasurer in Bavaria was a good example, with his position being confirmed by two men who stood on the Ecclesiastical Council, who made a lot of noise to ensure the appointment. All three were Illuminati men. Similarly, the Illuminati campaign against the Jesuits had always rumbled on. As their influence increased, a number of notable Jesuit institutions had been outlawed and banned, with the Jesuits themselves losing their grip on a number of academic institutions and positions within the Church. In the University of Ingolstadt, the once Jesuit-dominated teaching positions were put under pressure, with Illuminati members taking their place. It was almost inevitable that this level of influence would eventually result in jealousy and distrust among not only the Illuminati's rivals, but those who did not align with their beliefs.

To the public, it seemed as though the Illuminati were taking over the country. As we have seen, behind the scenes, things were far from perfect. But thanks to the nature of the secret society, only the tip of the iceberg was visible to the general public. While the visible elements of the Illuminati seemed to be a genuine concern, the members themselves were often arguing and in disagreement over what they should be doing in their pursuit of power. Such was the discord among the public that the authorities finally began to take notice of the growing Illuminati problem. The issue arrived at the feet of Karl Theodore, the person in charge of Bavaria. Facing increasing amounts of pressure, he was forced into actions.

His first move was to reinforce the ban on all of the secret societies. Though this had already been in place, the very existence of three difference groups (the Illuminati, the Freemasons, and the Rosicrucians, as well as many others) demonstrates that it was not rigorously enforced. As the tide of public opinion turned against the Illuminati, the order was given to clamp down on such groups, with special attention paid to the Illuminati. It was considered by some historians to be a "deathblow" to the Illuminati, with the Order unable to cope with the increased amount of attention and scrutiny that the government was placing on them. An edict, issued by the government and dated to the 2nd of March, 1785, made it clear that the Illuminati were specifically considered illegal.

The leading members within the Order could see quite clearly that they were not wanted. Though Bavaria had been their base of operations and the area from which they had risen up to their current position, many of the highest-ranking Illuminati men decided to flee. Weishaupt was one of the first, taking with him all of the documents, internal communications, letters, correspondence, and anything else he possessed that related to the secret society. However, these were seized in a number of operations between 1786 and 1787, and then they were published by the government in the same year. It provided a huge amount of insight into the formation of the Illuminati and can demonstrate to us the rise and fall of the Order as seen through its founder. But Weishaupt was not alone. A similar fate befell Von Zwack, who had his home raided and his documents seized. These were also published. Eventually, enough materials were gathered as to provide a good indication of exactly how the Illuminati had come into being.

The publishing of the internal communications can be read as the final death of the Illuminati. Though other events – Knigge leaving, the government edict – certainly signaled the end, it was the publishing of these materials that signaled the transition from secret society to strange relic of the past. The Illuminati's defining characteristic that they were a shadowy, secretive order was ripped away from them. The edifice of their abilities was torn down and the truth about their organization was made available for all to see. As well as making the communications visible for all to see, the publication had the effect of revealing many of the men who counted themselves as members of the Illuminati. Ferdinand of Brunswick was one such powerful figure, while Von

Zwack was an important diplomat at the time as well as being the second in command of the Illuminati. In addition, even famed artists and writers were implicated, including Johann Wolfgang von Goethe, the rulers of Gotha and Weimar, and Johann Gottfried Herder. It was more than enough to cause a scandal in Bavaria.

As the leaders of the organization fled the scene and the authorities systematically took apart the structure of the Illuminati, very little was left behind. Such was the perceived threat to the authorities that no stone was left unturned in the pursuit of the Order. Accordingly, the move essentially finished the Illuminati as a functioning, ambitious secret society. Though there might have been pockets of men who held out in the face of the Bavarians attempts to destroy the group, they were robbed of their ability to do very much at all. Groups such as the Freemasons began to look inwards and consider how the Illuminati had so easily infiltrated their Lodges. The governments began to scrutinize each and every influential position to a far greater level. Even though the Illuminati had succeeded in very little, their ability to rise up and become a threatening force in roughly a decade served as a wakeup call to those in power. While the Illuminati had died, their influence lived on.

But the real legacy of the Illuminati was much more difficult to grasp. Though the physical structures of the organization had been dismantled and all of their major players had fled, the name of the Illuminati lived on. Not only did it become famous in 18th Century Bavaria, but even today many people know the name. Ask anyone about a secret society and chances are the Illuminati will be one of the first names they mention. While the actual organization itself had died, the ghost of the Illuminati live on. In the next chapter, we will discuss how the ghost of such an organization could become such an influential and powerful name throughout the 18th, 19th, 20th, and even the 21st centuries.

The Illuminati Caused the French Revolution

After the fall of the Illuminati, the name lived on. Despite Weishaupt and his cohorts being forced to flee the scene and the entire organization being taken apart by the authorities, their reputation was such that they could easily be blamed for some of the more important events that were taking place around the world at this time. Locally, in Bavaria, many people were quick to attribute events that were slightly out of the ordinary on the Illuminati. Rulings in a court or changes in state policy would be accompanied by mutterings that perhaps some secret society was behind everything. As the disgraced organization that had been chased out of the country, the Illuminati were the logical choice on which to pin any kind of blame.

This is something which has continued to the modern day. Nowadays, there is a tendency to ascribe motivations to the most random of events. The rise of the conspiracy theorist has provided a subculture that questions every aspect of any event around the world. From the Moon landing to the events of September the 11th, 2001, there is always an alternative explanation. Typically, these involve shadowy conspiracies lurking in the background. In most circumstances, the name 'Illuminati' is well known enough to provide a suitable title for such a conspiracy. Even though we know the Bavarian Illuminati of Weishaupt is dead and gone, the name exists as a kind of go-to title for any makeshift conspiracy.

But this is not a new phenomenon. Shortly after the death of the Illuminati organization in Bavaria, events in France would have a huge impact on the world. The French Revolution was one of the single most important manifestations in Western history, leaving a legacy that can be said to include the rise of Napoleon, the First and Second World Wars, the Cold War, and everything we experience in our society today. In many ways, the slogan of "liberté, égalité, fraternité" came to embody the ideals that would drive the history of the next two centuries. In no short time at all, people noticed that the aims of the French Revolution were remarkably similar to the goals of the Illuminati and men like Weishaupt. It was barely any time at all before people were beginning to suggest that the Illuminati might have been responsible for events in France. But how did the organization come to be blamed for such a major moment in history?

The dates given for the French Revolution are typically between 1789 and 1799. During this period, civil unrest in France manifested itself in such a way as to encourage the people of France to rise up against the established order and overthrow the ruling aristocracy. The monarchy was dismantled, a French Republic established, and the groundwork eventually laid for a man named Napoleon to rise up and seize power. All of this was done under the banner of Enlightenment ideals. The liberal, somewhat radical views of men like Voltaire, combined with years of bad harvests, heavy taxation, and resentment of the clergy and aristocracy, led to an unprecedented uprising that shook the pillars of the European ruling classes. Built on Enlightenment ideas, it is possible to look at the views and opinions of Weishaupt and quietly assume the French Revolution must have been entirely to his liking.

This is exactly what seemed to have crossed the minds of a number of writers in Europe. In fact, two significant texts were published that suggested the Illuminati had not gone away. Instead, they had only appeared to do so and were, in fact, responsible for many world changing events, such as those seen in France. The books were *Proofs of a Conspiracy*, which was written by John Robison, and Augustin Barruel's book, titled *Memoirs Illustrating the History of Jacobinism*, published in 1798 and 1797 respectively. Though it's clear from the title alone that Robinson's book is hard at work in establishing a secret organization, Barruel's work functioned along very similar lines. Hardly a decade after the fall of the Illuminati, their name was essentially fair game to anyone who wanted to suggest the existence of a dangerous secret society. As the word Illuminati still carried some cultural cache, but the publication of the books were distant enough from the actual events, the authors were pretty much free to say whatever they pleased about the supposedly survival of the Illuminati.

Across both works, there is a conviction that the Illuminati never died. Ignoring the evidence of men such as Weishaupt and the events leading up to the disbanding of the organization, the two authors follow very similar paths in detailing the secret society. Both seem in agreement that the Illuminati simply withdrew from the public eye. Already a secret society, they seem to suggest that the Illuminati became a very secret society. From this positions way back in the shadows, the authors suggest that the group could organize events such as the French Revolution.

That both of the books sold well demonstrates the need people have to explain events in a simple, reductionist manner. Hundreds, possibly thousands of books have been written on the causes of the French Revolution. Historians and academics have long argued over what caused the uprising, providing Marxist readings of events, Psychoanalytic interpretations, and economic reasons why a group of disenfranchised people should fight against their overlords. But while modern historiography is more than capable of providing detailed reasoning behind events, it is a great deal easier to simply suggest that the Illuminati were behind everything. As the works of Robison and Barruel grew increasingly popular and the books were reprinted again and again, we can see for the first time how quickly people choose to accept the countercultural (and often easy) explanation rather than examining anything in great detail.

The two books inspired a wave of conspiracy related literature. For a while, many events were being blamed on the Illuminati, as well as other secret societies whose names have often been forgotten. As the French Revolution left a massive cultural impact on the Western world, there was an attempt to explain everything with a simple truth. Rather than believing that history could be a complex web of competing motivations and human emotions, the idea that a clandestine organization was in fact pulling the strings served to reduce everything to a very simple (though perhaps not desirable) explanation. It also had the effect of restoring order to a chaotic world. For those reading conspiracy literature at the time, the idea of events like the French Revolution occurring all over the world might seem worrisome. The French Revolution destroyed the working order, the established way of life. For those who were doing well for themselves, this kind of chaos was a threat. Having a shadowy group secretly pulling the strings applied a kind of rationale and order to the randomness of the French Revolution. Though they might not have agreed with the Illuminati's actions, there was some comfort to be found in the knowledge that someone, somewhere held the reins to this furious beast. In that respect, the idea of the Illuminati became much more important than the living organization had ever been.

But there were people at the time who were more than happy to dispel notions of a giant conspiracy across Europe. Some people happily bought into the idea and men such as Reverend Seth Payson wrote books like *Proofs of the Real Existence, and Dangerous Tendency, Of Illuminism* which purposefully described an Illuminati conspiracy. But the problem was, Payson and his like had no evidence. While they might have suggested that the Illuminati existed, there was little they could offer to back up their statements. This provided ample fodder for men like Jean-Joseph Mounier, who wrote a book titled *On the Influence Attributed to Philosophers, Free-Masons, and to the Illuminati on the Revolution of France*. Inside, he provided criticism of the ideas of the Illuminati conspiracy and was more than happy to dissuade people from this belief.

But such was the popularity of the idea that men like Barruel and Robison were able to make a large amount of money from the premise of a global conspiracy. They were able to travel to the newly formed country of America and give lectures and talks on how the Illuminati were influencing events. Much like Payson, they rarely had little in the way of definitive evidence. But it seemed not to matter. They were well paid for their writing and well paid for their work. They managed to influence others and, gradually, people like Jedidiah Morse (a priest) began to use the material as the foundation of his own ideas. These ideas were also printed, circulated, and built upon. Slowly, an entire genre of conspiratorial, speculative non-fiction began to spread across the world. At the heart of it all was the idea that groups such as the nominally defunct Illuminati were actually controlling global events.

But many of the salient facts got lost along the way. Much like a children's parlor game, in which a sentence is whispered into a series of ears until it metamorphoses into something entirely different, this idea of the Illuminati moved further and further away from the truth. While the initial books had succeeded in outlining the similarities between the principles of the French Revolution and the principles of the Illuminati, the derivative work became increasingly tenuous. Soon, the ideological foundations of such conspiracies vanished. In their stead was the modern interpretation of the Illuminati we see before us today. Rather than the liberal, radical group who sought to overthrow the monarchy and the church, the modern version of the Illuminati has become so twisted that these ideals are never mentioned. Instead, the Illuminati are a ruling elite, or focused on enslaving humanity, or hoping to use Israel to topple the world, or they are behind the global banking crises. With very little effort, it is possible to find someone who has attributed almost any political event from the last century to the work of the Illuminati.

So while the Illuminati in no way were responsible for the French Revolution, the possibility that they might have guided events has become one of the most important moments in the organization's history. These days, the ghost of the Illuminati is an entirely different beast. As we will see in the final chapter, the modern Illuminati can be traced back to the conspiracy theories that plagued the French Revolution. Soon enough, we'll find the final truth behind the Illuminati myth.

The Illuminati in Modern Society

These days, the word "Illuminati" is basically a brand name. Utterly divorced from the secret society origins that rose up in Bavaria in the 18th Century, the group have been co-opted by everyone from college fraternities to fiction writers, from internet conspiracy theorists to video game creators. Through all of these iterations, the true history of the organization is often lost, forgotten, or simply ignored completely. If we want to question the idea of the Illuminati in the modern day, then we need to understand that the meaning of the word is entirely different. While we have looked in depth at the Bavarian origins of the Illuminati, this understanding shows us just how separate from the truth the contemporary uses of the group have become.

It is not uncommon to see the Illuminati inspire those who are looking to set up their own secret society. Having become the default title for any kind of shadowy organization, many organizations that are keen to emphasize their own importance will take the Illuminati as a starting point. Whether this means adding some variation of the name – the Illuminated, Illumination, Illuminate, and so on – or even borrowing some of the Order's iconography – the Minerval owl, for example – there are many examples of people who hope to give their own group credibility by invoking the Illuminati. These might be Masonic sects, college fraternities, or just curious people getting together to meet in private. All of them are aware, at least on some level, of what the name Illuminati means. They are very rarely aware, however, of what the Order stood for.

In a similar vein, there are many works of fiction that choose to use the Illuminati as a plot device. Established fiction authors such as Dan Brown (author of the *Da Vinci Code* and *Angels and Demons*) and Umberto Eco (*Foucault's Pendulum*) have both sold a great many novels while featuring characters who were in some way related to the Illuminati. Across everything from children's books, to movies, to video games, the Illuminati can be a very useful plot device. Thanks to their reputation, they spark a kind of instant familiarity, especially useful as the authors can adjust the group's motivations depending on the particular story. These days, many people's first exposure to the word 'Illuminati' will come from works of fiction such as these, created by writers whose research can vary from the incredibly in-depth to the casual and cursory. With so many different forms of media depicting the Illuminati, the ghost of the Bavarian secret society has taken on a new life as a recurring organization in fiction, much like the United Nations or NASA.

The prevalence of the Illuminati across many forms of fiction can often form the starting point for people's understanding of the group, but it is very rarely the ending point. Once people hear the name, they often have their interests piqued and become curious about what the group is about. Inevitably, they will take to the internet. Simply typing the word "Illuminati" into a search engine will provide the user with 25,000,000 results. On twenty-five million webpages, all across the internet, someone has mentioned the Illuminati. Giving a quick glance down the first page of results, the authenticity of the research quickly becomes questionable. Very soon, the questions move away from historical and verifiable facts and towards questions of whether the Illuminati control the music industry, of whether they influence celebrities, or whether their logo is featured on American currency. Such matters are as entirely divorced from the original Illuminati as to be something else entirely.

Take, for example, the myth that the Illuminati feature on the one dollar bill of the United States of America. According to the legend, the following can be found on the note:

- The Illuminated eye floating atop the pyramid, which is said to represent Lucifer the Great Architect. The eye was never a symbol of the Illuminati, and their relation to the occult and the mystical was inconsistent at best, far from their reputation as devil worshipers.
- The pyramid features 13 layers of bricks, which represent the original 13 colonies of America and 72 bricks to represent the 72 powers of the Kabbalistic name of God. The Illuminati had no presence in America, certainly not during the founding of the country, and any kind of belief in Jewish mysticism can be considered ridiculous, as Jews were barred from joining.
- The date MDCCLXXVI, which represents the day the Illuminati were formed – ignoring the auspicious nature of that date in term of American history, the Illuminati name was not invented for an additional two years.
- The prevalence of the number 13, connected to paganism and power over the thirteen colonies – paganism was at odds with the rational nature of the Illuminati mindset.

There are many more websites that claim that almost every aspect of the one dollar bill (and others) hints at the Illuminati and how they secretly control America. Conspiracy theories such as this are not only the most common use of the word Illuminati in the modern age, but they represent an ill-informed and often purposefully ignorant interpretation of the history of the Order. Even the most cursory research can eliminate the minor details and suggestions put forward by these websites. What's more, few of the theorists are able to answer the question as to why a secret society would declare their existence on one of the most common items in the country. If the Illuminati wanted to keep their existence a secret, then it is unlikely that they would advertise on the country's currency. Furthermore, if they did indeed leave coded messages, their codes could likely stand up to a greater amount of scrutiny that making vague associations.

Instead, these websites perform the essential modern function of the Illuminati in our culture. The millions of sites that claim to possess knowledge of the conspiratorial trends of a modern Illuminati simply trade on the famous nature of the name in return for attention. It can help to think of the usage of the name like a franchise. Just like with a fast food chain, a person takes the name and puts it above their door. The name carries certain connotations for the viewer, who knows what they can expect when they go inside. Just as a fast food customer can expect the same kind of burgers across the country, those who wander into the more dubious areas of the internet which fix the word Illuminati above their door know what to expect. And just like in fast food restaurants, the people cooking the food are entirely different. While it might be the same name above the door, the people inside are far from the original workers. Today, the Illuminati name carries a certain cultural meaning but very little else.

So why does the name remain important? As well as the fascination some people have with the idea of conspiracy theories, one of the most important explanations for the popularity of the Illuminati is simple. Money. By putting the word Illuminati in the title of a book, one can expect to sell more copies. Put the organization into a film or video game and people will know what to expect. Mention it on the internet and people will eventually arrive at your site. Rather than a global conspiracy, the popularity of the Illuminati in the modern age can typically be attributed to cold, hard cash.

It is telling that men such as Mark Dice or David Icke are able to trade so freely on the Illuminati name. Often paying very little attention to the organization's Bavarian origins, they play on the modern conception of the Order. There is a huge amount of money to be made from people's inquisitive natures. The audience wants to know the secret, the solution, the key to how everything works. While the real answers to these questions are often infinitesimally correct, packaging up a simple answer can be immensely profitable. By claiming that the Illuminati are some modern global puppet masters, it is possible to provide an alternative explanation that is ever so slightly plausible, much easier to comprehend, and almost impossible to prove right or wrong. Just as the Illuminati have become a brand name for bland conspiracy theories, they have become a profitable venture. Read almost any text on the subject and there will be little mention of the original Enlightenment ideals behind the group, or the discussions between Knigge and Weishaupt. Instead, discussion drifts to celebrity encounters, half-hearted iconographic explanations, and thorough misinterpretations of actual history. Evidence is ignored, and in its place is a titillating, tempting alternative. A truth that could be true, but that will never be proved. Today, the Illuminati are dead and gone. In their place, a modern ghost of the Order has risen up and become a profitable, entertaining option for anyone who wants to believe in the possibility of a conspiracy.

Conclusion

Many people will pick up a book on the Illuminati with the hope that it will explain any number of conspiracy theories. Did they assassinate JFK? Did they organize the Bolshevik revolution? Were they behind any number of terrorist attacks, horrible accidents, and other world changing events? The answer is almost invariably "no." In this book, we have attempted to explain why.

There exists two very different versions of the Illuminati. The is the factual version, the secret society that was founded in 18th Century Bavaria, that has left a legacy of evidence, materials, and historical provable facts. And there is the fiction, the ensuing interpretation of the Illuminati that makes them both everything and nothing. They are simultaneously responsible for the greatest conspiracy every put into practice, while clandestine enough to leave no evidence whatsoever. The modern version is a ghost story, built from the blocks of the historical Order than crumbled under its own failings.

The real Illuminati was an ambitious, radical, and liberal organization. It was eventually torn apart by very human failings and the age-old inability of individuals to reach a consensus. It's possible to see very normal, sympathetic traits in the history of the Bavarian Illuminati. But the modern version provides us with an equal insight into the human condition. The Illuminati as we know them today offer answers in a world full of questions. They offer some semblance of explanation when the facts desert us. For those who believe in their actions, the Illuminati become a way to explain the inexplicable. While this does not make the stories true, it at least explains why the Illuminati continue to exist and will carry on existing for the foreseeable future.

Further Reading

Black, J. (2010). *The secret history of the world*. London: Quercus.

Dice, M. (n.d.). *Inside the Illuminati*.

Illuminati in the Music Industry. (2013). Createspace Independent Pub.

Illuminatiam. (n.d.). .

Jackson, J. (2015). *The World's Most Dangerous Secret Societies*. Createspace.

Makow, H. (2009). *Illuminati*. Winnipeg, MB: Silas Green.

Satanic Possession. (2014). Createspace Independent Pub.

The 66 laws of the Illuminati. (n.d.). .

White, F. (n.d.). *Who are the Illuminati?*.

Zagami, L. (2016). *Confessions of an illuminati*. [Place of publication not identified]: Ccc Pub.

Image Credits

1. Adam Weishaupt - Source: Author unknown. Public domain.

2. Adolph Freiherr Knigge - Source: Author unknown. Public domain.

3. Scan of Illuminati pamphlet from 1788. Creative commons licence.

4. Freemasons' Hall – 1809 - Thomas Rowlandson (1756–1827) and Augustus Charles Pugin (1762–1832) (after) John Bluck (fl. 1791–1819), Joseph Constantine Stadler (fl. 1780–1812), Thomas Sutherland (1785–1838), J. Hill, and Harraden (aquatint engravers)

5. T. Schweighart, Speculum sophicum Rhodostauroticum (1604)

6. Eugène Delacroix - Liberty Leading the People – 1830

7. Scan of one dollar bill from United States of America

Excerpt from Conrad Bauer's book The Priory of Sion: Hoax, Conspiracy, or Secret Society

Hoax, conspiracy, or secret society? That is the range of responses you might hear when raising the idea of the Priory of Sion. Ostensibly a clandestine order designed to disguise the truth about the children of Jesus Christ, the group have been labeled as either an elaborate concoction, or the most powerful secret society in the world. Are they real? What are they hiding? Where did they come from? What impact can they have on the world around us? These are the questions this book will hope to answer.

At the heart of the story of the Priory of Sion is the somewhat heretical notion that Jesus Christ — the supposed son of God — fathered children. Not only that, but that his bloodline survives to this day. If true, the idea has a huge impact on the very existence of Christianity, the world's most popular religion. If the Priory — as is believed — are guarding the truth about such a matter, they then potentially control some of the most powerful information in the world. Think of it like an ideological atomic bomb, ticking away and ready to explode through the consciousness of the world.

Not only that, but the men allegedly chosen to guard these secrets rank as some of the greatest thinkers in human history. Isaac Newton, Nicholas Flamel, and Leonardo da Vinci have all been implicated in the order, though their involvement is debated. In fact, the entire existence of the order has been argued. Some suggest that, rather than a secret society, the Priory is in fact an elaborate hoax.

Others claim that these accusations are merely an attempt to disguise the truth. But what do we know for certain? Who exactly are the Priory of Sion?

Hidden Evidence

One of the most important parts of this story is a battle. On one side is an American, pressed into defending himself. On the other side, three Englishmen stand convinced that they have been robbed and their ideas made to seem ridiculous. It is as though their honor has been sullied. They demand satisfaction. Each side is spending hundreds of thousands of dollars to face off against the other and it will not be settled until one side emerges victorious. But rather than some medieval fist fight or Victorian duel, this is a very recent battle. Though the history of the Priory of Sion is said to stretch back for thousands of years, this fight was fought after the turn of the second millennium. The venue is the Royal Courts of Justice in a part of London known as the Strand. The date is 2006.

This is where we will start. These days, it is impossible to discuss the Priory of Sion without mentioning a number of books. These books vary in popularity, from an international bestseller which made its author millions, through to a supposedly academic work which defied expectations and left a print on the world, and finally, an obscure French text, one which many people have credited with starting this entire affair. Appropriately enough for a story that may or may not be true, the publishing of books is inextricably linked to the Priory in every single respect. As we shall see, the writing, the reading, and the impact of these texts is essential to the story.

Of these books, two were written by the men who stood opposed to one another in the Strand. On one side was Dan Brown, writer of *The Da Vinci Code*, and the man often credited with turning the Priory of Sion into a global concern. Condemned by the Church, ridiculed by critics, his work has nevertheless proved to be a success beyond any comprehension. For the university professor, it has become a rich industry. As someone who teaches other to write, there are few people in the world better placed to tell others how to make money from a story. But how that story came to be is the entire predicament of the court case.

On the other side of the courtroom stand two men and their team of lawyers. Richard Leigh, hailing from New Jersey, and Michael Baigent, hailing from New Zealand. They glower at Dan Brown (who, strangely enough, hails from New Hampshire) from the other side of Court 61. Dan Brown is the defendant and the other two men have accused him of plagiarism. Brown, they say, not only stole their ideas, but presented them to the world in a way which discredited the work they had done. Baigent and Leigh are better known to the world as the authors of *The Holy Blood and the Holy Grail*. As well as being one of the most popular pieces of writing ever created on the subject of the Holy Grail, their book brings the idea of the Priory of Sion to an English-speaking audience. As we will discover soon, their work was wildly successful and few writers have come as close to delivering as ground-breaking, as controversial, and as profitable a take on religion in the last three centuries.

And so both sides of the courtroom are inhabited by writers. On this day, a verdict is to be reached which will lend credence to (or demolish the credibility of) an idea which is said to date back almost 2,000 years. At the heart of the matter, with the judge set to rule, is the purported existence of the Priory of Sion. Through the works of both sides of the argument, the Priory's name has reached more ears than anyone ever thought possible. While Brown has managed to dominate the bestseller charts in the world of fiction, Baigent and Leigh (as well as a third author who is not present, but who will be touched upon soon) created massive waves in the world of non-fiction. Between them, they have dominated both sides of the bestseller charts.

That is one of the key underlying aspects of the case and, by extension, the existence of the Priory of Sion itself. There is a huge amount of money to be made in publishing these ideas. Whether that is because they are dangerous, because they are revelatory, or because they are entertaining, is never really made clear. But, simply because the case ever came to court, there is money to be made through publishing works on the Priory of Sion. And, with court cases such as these, there is also a huge amount of money to be lost.

So what exactly were the duo of Baigent and Leigh claiming in Courtroom 61? Their case was not as simple as run-of-the-mill plagiarism. Typically, in plagiarism cases, the prosecution must prove that the defendant took their idea and made a profit on it, without attributing credit or sharing in the revenue. This has been done countless times in the past and, in the world of publishing (and the media at large) it is not uncommon. But this particular case was slightly different.

Specifically, Baigent and Leigh claimed that Brown — in *The Da Vinci Code* — made use of a plot that was "directly plagiarized" from their own book, *The Holy Blood and the Holy Grail*. Stealing this idea, they said, allowed Brown to make a huge amount of money from the ideas of the original authors. At the time of the court case, it was estimated that Brown's writing had made him in excess of $45 million. Besides the book, there was the multi-million dollar film franchise starring Tom Hanks. *The Da Vinci Code* had achieved huge success, ranking perhaps alongside Harry Potter alone in terms of post-millennial publishing successes. This success, the prosecution alleged, was built on top of ideas that were borrowed wholesale from *The Holy Blood and the Holy Grail*.

That is not to say that *The Holy Blood and the Holy Grail* had not been successful in its own right. Far from it. Indeed, after being published in the 1980s, the book caused a huge stir. But it was considered (by both its authors and its readership) as a work of non-fiction. Walk into any bookshop in a quest for the book and it would be found in the non-fiction section. Indeed, rather than the new age or the spirituality section, *The Holy Blood and the Holy Grail* was nestled amid other, weightier works under the banner of history. This was the realm in which the book dominated. Most non-fiction books do not sell in huge numbers, but this one was different. Perhaps because it managed to transition from the speculative theology that most people dismiss, into the realms of accepted historicism, it had become immensely popular.

And herein lay the rub. For the authors of *The Holy Blood and the Holy Grail*, the very existence of *The Da Vinci Code* undermined their own work. Not only were ideas borrowed from the historical text, but they were presented in a fictional world, and this brought them into question. Convinced as they were that the Priory of Sion was a real, functioning body, the way in which Dan Brown had taken and presented his ideas undid all of the work they had achieved to that point. Their future successes (and the successes of the sequels to *The Holy Blood and the Holy Grail*) were damaged by the existence of *The Da Vinci Code*. This was why they were suing.

To that point, it almost seemed as though money was far from the issue. Baigent, Leigh, and Henry Lincoln (the third writer) had already become wealthy men. Their years of research into what had eventually become *The Holy Blood and the Holy Grail* had turned them from struggling writers into authorities on the Holy Grail and, in particular, the Priory of Sion. Michael Baigent was even quoted at the time as having said, "Whether our hypothesis is right or wrong is irrelevant." The lawsuit was not an attempted to earn punitive damages, but to protect their ideas, to protect their integrity, and to protect the idea of the Priory of Sion. As Baigent stated, the authors felt as though they had "no choice."

Baigent and Leigh resented "being lumped in" with the work of fiction known as *The Da Vinci Code*. As they constantly insisted in the press, it seemed more and more as though this was indeed a high-minded quest to protect their intellectual property in the face of an overwhelming behemoth of the fictional world. It was almost as though these men were the protectors of the integrity of the Priory of Sion, holding out against the bastardized version that had been presented to the world by the callous Dan Brown. As anyone in the publishing world will tell you, a non-fiction bestseller (such as *The Holy Blood and the Holy Grail*) might net plaudits and respect, but a fiction bestseller (such as *The Da Vinci Code*) will always net you the profits. So while Baigent and Leigh were keen to protect their integrity and that of their work, Dan Brown and his publishers were very keen to keep their money-making avenues open. And so there the men found themselves, facing off against one another in a London courtroom.

Key to Baigent's argument (and that of his legal team) was the idea of "historical implication." *The Holy Blood and the Holy Grail*, the authors argued, was an authoritative historical text. It was one that they had spent years researching and putting together. *The Da Vinci Code*, if read by millions, damaged the implied historical accuracy of the non-fiction work. It was not quite plagiarism, but it was the argument that Baigent repeated time and time again in the press.

But the idea seemed to fly in the face of common sense. Surely, if a reader sat down with either book, they would naturally know that one was a work of fiction and the other was a work of non-fiction? The tone, presentation, style, and even the cover of the book would tell them as much. As long as *The Da Vinci Code* veered away from quoting verbatim tracts of the other text without crediting it, how could this "historical implication" affect *The Holy Blood and the Holy Grail*?

Furthermore, if the alleged history told by the authors of *The Holy Blood and the Holy Grail* was indeed held to be true, the facts should have been available to a fiction writer regardless of whether they appeared in a particular book or not. When writing about the past, school textbook writers rarely take authors to court over the mention of the Battle of Hastings or the Spanish Inquisition. If the book written by Baigent and his co-writers was based purely on fact (as is the premise in non-fiction) then there seemed little wrong with Dan Brown making use of an idea such as the Priory of Sion, and the secrets they guarded.

About the Author

Conrad Bauer is passionate about everything paranormal, unexplained, mysterious, and terrifying. It comes from his childhood and the famous stories his grandfather used to tell the family during summer vacation camping trips. He vividly remembers his grandfather sitting around the fire with new stories to tell everyone who would gather around and listen. His favorites were about the paranormal, including ghost stories, haunted houses, strange places, and paranormal occurrences.

Bauer is an adventurous traveler who has gone to many places in search of the unexplained and paranormal. He has been researching the paranormal and what scares people for more than four decades. He also loves to dig into period of history that are still full of mysteries, being an avid reader of the mystic secret societies that have mark history and remain fascinating and legendary throughout the times. He has accumulated a solid expertise and knowledge that he now shares through his books with his readers and followers.

Conrad, now retired, lives in the countryside in Ireland with his wife and two dogs.

More Books from Conrad Bauer

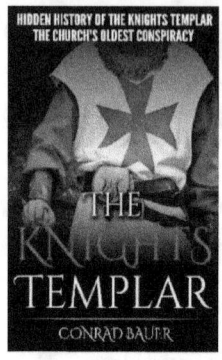  

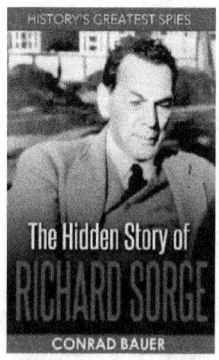  

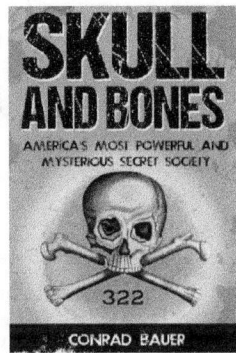